50 Ripple Stitches™

Defined Ripples

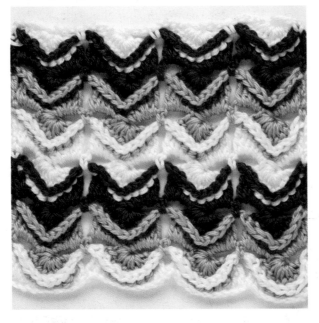

PATTERN NOTES
This uses 3 or more colors.

Chain-4 at beginning of row or round counts as first treble crochet unless otherwise stated.

SPECIAL STITCH
Front post double crochet decrease (fpdc dec): Holding back last lp of each st on hook, **fpdc** (*see Stitch Guide*) around st indicated in instructions, yo, pull through all lps on hook.

INSTRUCTIONS
Row 1 (RS): With first color, ch a multiple of 11 plus 15, tr in 5th ch from hook (*first 4 chs count as first tr*), tr in next ch, dc in each of next 2 chs, hdc in each of next 2 chs, dc in each of next 2 chs, tr in each of next 2 chs, *ch 2, sk next ch, tr in each of next 2 chs, dc in each of next 2 chs, hdc in each of next 2 chs, dc in each of next 2 chs, tr in each of next 2 chs, rep from * across, tr in last st, turn. Fasten off.

Row 2: Join next color with sc in first st, *ch 4, **fpdc dec** (*see Special Stitch*) around next 10 sts, ch 4**, sc in next ch-2 sp, rep from * across, ending last rep at **, sc in last st, turn.

Row 3: **Ch 4** (*see Pattern Notes*), *(2 tr, 2 dc, 2 hdc) in next ch-4 sp, (2 hdc, 2 dc, 2 tr) in next ch-4 sp**, ch 2, rep from * across, ending last rep at **, tr in last st, turn. Fasten off.

Rep rows 2 and 3 alternately for pattern, working 2 rows of each color. ■

Double Tripled

PATTERN NOTES
This uses 3 colors.

Join with slip stitch as indicated unless otherwise stated.

Chain-3 at beginning of row or round counts as first double crochet unless otherwise stated.

INSTRUCTIONS
Row 1 (RS): With first color, ch a multiple of 29 plus 30, 2 dc in 5th ch from hook (*first 4 chs count as first dc and sk ch*), *[sk next ch, 2 dc in next ch] 5 times, sk next ch, (2 dc, ch 3, 2 dc)

in next ch, sk next ch, [2 dc in next ch, sk next ch] 5 times**, 2 dc in next ch, sk next 4 chs, 2 dc in next ch, rep from * across, ending last rep at **, sk next ch, 3 dc in last ch, turn. Fasten off.

Row 2: **Join** *(see Pattern Notes)* next color in first st, **ch 3** *(see Pattern Notes)*, sk next dc, dc in sp between last dc and next dc, [sk next 2 dc, 2 dc in sp between last dc and next dc] 6 times, *(2 dc, ch 3, 2 dc) in next ch sp, sk next dc, 2 dc in sp between last dc and next dc, [sk next 2 dc, 2 dc in sp between last dc and next dc] 5 times**, sk next 6 dc, dc in sp between last dc and next dc, [sk next 2 dc, 2 dc in sp between last dc and next dc] 5 times, rep from * across, ending last rep at **, sk next 2 dc, dc in sp between last dc and next dc, dc in last st, turn.

Rep row 2 for pattern, changing to next color on each row. ∎

Snow Berries

PATTERN NOTES
This uses 2 colors.

Join with slip stitch as indicated unless otherwise stated.

SPECIAL STITCH
Puff stitch (puff st): [Yo, insert hook as indicated in instructions, yo, pull up lp] 3 times, yo, pull through all lps on hook.

INSTRUCTIONS
Row 1 (RS): With first color, ch a multiple of 23 plus 24, **sc dec** *(see Stitch Guide)* in 2nd and 3rd chs from hook, ch 2, *[sk next ch, **puff st** *(see Special Stitch)* in next ch, ch 2] 4 times, sk next ch, (puff st, ch 2, puff st) in next ch, [ch 2, sk next ch, puff st in next ch] 4 times, sk next ch**, puff st in next ch, sk next 2 chs, puff st in next ch, rep from * across, ending last rep at **, sc dec in last 2 chs, turn. Fasten off.

Row 2: **Join** *(see Pattern Notes)* next color in first st, ch 1, hdc in next ch-2 sp, *ch 2, [hdc in next ch-2 sp, ch 2] 4 times, (hdc, ch 2, hdc) in next ch-2 sp, [ch 2, hdc in next ch-2 sp] 4 times, ch 2**, **hdc dec** *(see Stitch Guide)* in next 2 ch-2 sps, rep from * across, ending last rep at **, hdc dec in last ch-2 sp and last st, turn. Fasten off.

Row 3: Join first color in first st, ch 1, sc dec in same st and ch-2 sp, *[puff st in next ch-2 sp, ch 2] 4 times, (puff st, ch 2, puff st) in next ch-2 sp, ch 2, [puff st in next ch-3 sp, ch 2] 4 times**, puff st in each of next ch-2 sps, rep from * across, ending last rep at **, sc dec in last ch-2 sp and last st, turn. Fasten off.

Row 4: Join next color in first st, ch 1, hdc in next ch-2 sp, *ch 2, [hdc in next ch-2 sp, ch 2] 4 times, (hdc, ch 2, hdc) in next ch-2 sp, [ch 2, hdc in next ch-2 sp] 4 times, ch 2**, hdc dec in next 2 ch-2 sps, rep from * across, ending last rep at **, hdc dec in last ch-2 sp and last st, turn.

Rows 5–10: Ch 1, hdc in next ch-2 sp, *ch 2, [hdc in next ch-2 sp, ch 2] 4 times, (hdc, ch 2, hdc) in next ch-2 sp, [ch 2, hdc in next ch-2 sp] 4 times, ch 2**, hdc dec in next 2 ch-2 sps, rep from * across, ending last rep at **, hdc dec in last ch-2 sp and last st, turn.

Row 11: Rep row 3.

Rep rows 2–11 consecutively for pattern, ending with first color and row 3. ∎

Unexpected

PATTERN NOTES
This uses 1 color.

Chain-3 at beginning of row or round counts as first double crochet unless otherwise stated.

Chain-2 at beginning of row or round **does not** count as first stitch unless otherwise stated.

SPECIAL STITCH
Decrease (dec): Holding back last lp of each st on hook, dc in next st, sk dc dec, dc in next dc, yo, pull through all lps on hook.

INSTRUCTIONS
Row 1: Ch a multiple of 31 plus 29, dc in 4th ch from hook, dc in each of next 11 chs, *(2 dc, ch 2, 2 dc) in next ch, dc in each of next 12 chs**, sk next 2 chs, **dc dec** *(see Stitch Guide)* in next 2 chs, sk next 2 chs, dc in each of next 12 chs, rep from * across, ending last rep at **, dc in last st, turn.

Row 2 (RS): Ch 3 *(see Pattern Notes)*, dc dec in next 2 sts, [sk next st, dc in next st, working in front of dc just made, **fpdc** *(see Stitch Guide)* around st just sk] 6 times, *(2 dc, ch 2, 2 dc) in next ch-2 sp, [sk next dc, dc in next dc, working in front of dc just made, fpdc around dc just sk] 6 times**, sk next st, **dec** *(see Special Stitch)*, s k next st, [sk next st, dc in next dc, working in front of last dc made, fpdc around st just sk] 6 times, rep from * across, ending last rep at **, dc dec in last 3 sts, turn.

Row 3: Ch 2 *(see Pattern Notes)*, dc dec in next 2 sts, *dc in each of next 12 sts, (2 dc, ch 2, 2 dc) in next ch-2 sp, dc in each of next 12 sts**, sk next st, dec, sk next st, rep from * across, ending last rep at **, dc dec in last 3 sts, turn.

Rep rows 2 and 3 alternately for pattern, ending with row 2. ∎

Bodacious

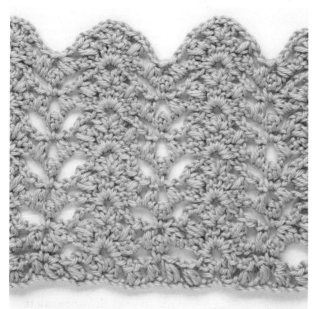

PATTERN NOTES
This uses 1 color.

Chain-3 at beginning of row or round counts as first double crochet unless otherwise stated.

Chain-4 at beginning of row or round counts as first double crochet and chain-1 unless otherwise stated.

SPECIAL STITCHES
Cluster (cl): Holding back last lp of each st on hook, 2 dc as indicated in instructions, yo, pull through all lps on hook.

Small shell (sm shell): (2 dc, ch 1, 2 dc) as indicated in instructions.

Large shell (lg shell): (Dc, {ch 2, dc} 6 times) as indicated in instructions.

Picot: Ch 3, sl st in top of last st worked.

INSTRUCTIONS
Row 1 (RS): Ch a multiple of 15 plus 19, 2 dc in 4th ch from hook (*first 3 chs count as first dc*), *[ch 2, sk next 2 chs, **cl** (*see Special Stitches*) in next ch] 4 times**, sk next 2 chs, **sm shell** (*see Special Stitches*) in next ch, rep from * across, ending last rep at **, sk next 2 chs, 3 dc in last ch, turn.

Row 2: Ch 4 (*see Pattern Notes*), (dc, ch 1, dc) in same st, *ch 3, sk next ch sp, next cl, next ch sp and next cl, sc in next ch-2 sp, **picot** (*see Special Stitches*), ch 3**, **lg shell** (*see Special Stitches*) in ch sp of next sm shell, sk all sts and ch sps between, rep from * across, ending last rep at **, (dc, {ch 1, dc} twice) in last st, turn.

Row 3: Ch 3 (*see Pattern Notes*), 2 dc in same st, *ch 2, sk next ch-1 sp, cl in next ch-1 sp, ch 2, cl in each of next 2 ch-3 sps, ch 2, sk next ch-1 sp, cl in next ch-1 sp, ch 2**, sk next ch-1 sp, sm shell in next dc, rep from * across, ending last rep at **, cl in next ch-1 sp, sk next ch-1 sp, 3 dc in last st, turn.

Rep rows 2 and 3 alternately for pattern. ■

Valiant

PATTERN NOTES

This uses 3 colors.

Join with slip stitch as indicated unless otherwise stated.

Chain-3 at beginning of row or round counts as first double crochet unless otherwise stated.

INSTRUCTIONS

Row 1 (RS): With first color, ch a multiple of 16 plus 20, 2 dc in 4th ch from hook (*first 3 chs count as first dc*), *dc in each of next 5 chs, **dc dec** (*see Stitch Guide*) in next 5 chs, dc in each of next 5 chs**, 5 dc in next ch, rep from * across, ending last rep at **, 3 dc in last ch, turn. Fasten off.

Row 2: **Join** (*see Pattern Notes*) next color, **ch 3** (*see Pattern Notes*), 2 dc in same st, *[ch 1, sk next dc, dc in next dc] twice, ch 1, sk next dc, dc dec in next 5 dc, [ch 1, sk next dc, dc in next dc] twice, ch 1, sk next dc**, 5 dc in next dc, rep from * across, ending last rep at **, 3 dc in last st, turn. Fasten off.

Row 3: Join next color with sc in first st, sc in each of next 2 sts, *working over ch sp, dc in sk st below, [sc in next dc, working over ch sp, dc in next sk st below] twice, sc in next dc dec, working over ch sp, dc in sk st below, [sc in next dc, working over ch sp, dc in next sk st below] twice**, sc in each of next 5 dc, rep from * across, ending last rep at **, sc in each of last 3 sts, turn. Fasten off.

Row 4: Rep row 2.

Row 5: Working in sts and in ch sps, join first color in first st, ch 3, 2 dc in same st, *dc in each of next 5 sts, dc dec in next 5 sts, dc in each of next 5 sts**, 5 dc in next st, rep from * across, ending last rep at **, 3 dc in last st, turn. Fasten off.

Rep rows 2–5 consecutively for pattern. ■

Curliques

PATTERN NOTES
This uses 3 colors.

Join with slip stitch as indicated unless
otherwise stated.

Chain-2 at beginning of row or round **does not**
count as first stitch unless otherwise stated.

SPECIAL STITCH
Curlique: Sl st around sc dec below next sc dec,
ch 6, 3 sc in 2nd ch from hook and in each ch
across, sl st around same dc dec.

INSTRUCTIONS
Row 1 (RS): Ch a multiple of 18 plus 20, dc in
3rd ch from hook (*first 2 chs do not count as first
st*), dc in each of next 7 chs, *3 dc in next ch,
dc in each of next 7 chs**, **dc dec** (*see Stitch
Guide*) in next 3 chs, dc in each of next 7 chs,
rep from * across, ending last rep at **, dc dec
in last 2 chs, turn.

Rows 2–6: **Ch 2** (*see Pattern Notes*), dc in next st,
***bpdc** (*see Stitch Guide*) around next st, [**fpdc**
(*see Stitch Guide*) around next st, bpdc around
next st] 3 times, 3 dc in next st, bpdc around
next st, [fpdc around next st, bpdc around next
st] 3 times**, dc dec in next 3 sts, rep from *
across, ending last rep at **, dc dec in last 2 sts,
turn. Fasten off.

Row 7: **Join** (*see Pattern Notes*) next color in first
st, **sc dec** (*see Stitch Guide*) in same st and next
st, *sc in each of next 7 sts, 3 sc in next st, sc
in each of next 7 sts**, sc dec in next 3 sts, rep
from * across, ending last rep at **, sc dec in last
2 sts, turn.

Row 8: Ch 1, sc dec in first 2 sts, *sc in each
of next 7 sts, 3 sc in next st, sc in each of next
7 sts**, sc dec in next 3 sts, rep from * across,
ending last rep at **, sc dec in last 2 sts, turn.
Fasten off.

Row 9: Join next color in first st, sc dec in same
st and next st, sc in each of next 7 sts, *3 sc in
next st, sc in each of next 7 sts**, sk next st,
curlique (*see Special Stitch*), sk next st, sc in
each of next 7 sts, rep from * across, ending last
rep at **, sc dec in last 2 sts, turn.

Row 10: Ch 1, sc dec in first 2 sts, sc in each
of next 7 sts, *3 sc in next st, sc in each of next
7 sts**, sc dec in sc before and sc after curlique,
sc in each of next 7 sts, rep from * across,
ending last rep at **, sc dec in last 2 sts, turn.
Fasten off.

Rows 11 & 12: Rep rows 7 and 8 with same
color used in rows 7 and 8.

Row 13: Join first color in first st, ch 2, dc in
next st, dc in each of next 7 sts, *3 dc in next st,
dc in each of next 7 sts**, dc dec in next 3 sts,
dc in each of next 7 sts, rep from * across,
ending last rep at **, ending with dc dec in
last 2 sts, turn.

Rep rows 2–13 consecutively for pattern, ending
with row 6. ■

Glacier Peaks

PATTERN NOTES
This uses 5 colors.

Join with slip stitch as indicated unless otherwise stated.

SPECIAL STITCH
Decrease (dec): Insert hook in next ch or st, yo, pull lp through, sk next 2 chs or sts, insert hook in next ch or st, yo, pull lp through, yo, pull through all lps on hook.

INSTRUCTIONS
Row 1 (RS): With first color, ch a multiple of 11 plus 11, sc in 2nd ch from hook, *ch 2, sk next ch, sc in next ch, ch 2, sk next ch, (sc, ch 2, sc) in next ch, ch 2, sk next ch, sc in next ch, ch 2,

sk next ch**, **dec** *(see Special Stitch)*, rep from * across, ending last rep at **, **sc dec** *(see Stitch Guide)* in last 2 chs, turn.

Row 2: Ch 1, sc dec in first st and next ch-2 sp, *ch 2, sc in next ch-2 sp, ch 2, (sc, ch 2, sc) in next ch-2 sp, ch 2, sc in next ch-2 sp, ch 2**, sc dec in next 2 ch-2 sps at dec, rep from * across, ending last rep at **, sc dec in last ch-2 sp and last st, turn.

Rows 3–8: Rep row 2. At end of last row, fasten off.

Row 9: **Join** *(see Pattern Notes)* next color in first st, ch 1, sk first st, hdc in next ch-2 sp, ch 1, 2 hdc in next ch-2 sp, ch 1, *(hdc, ch 2, hdc) in next ch-2 sp**, [ch 1, 2 hdc in next ch-2 sp] twice, (2 hdc in next ch-2 sp, ch 1] twice, rep from * across, ending last rep at **, ch 1, 2 hdc in next ch-2 sp, ch 1, **hdc dec** *(see Stitch Guide)* in last ch-2 sp and last st, turn. Fasten off.

Row 10: Join next color in first st, ch 1, sk first st, hdc in next ch-1 sp, ch 1, 2 hdc in next ch-1 sp, ch 1, *(hdc, ch 2, hdc) in next ch-2 sp**, [ch 1, 2 hdc in next ch-1 sp] twice, [2 hdc in next ch-1 sp, ch 1] twice, rep from * across, ending last rep at **, ch 1, 2 hdc in next ch-1 sp, ch 1, hdc dec in last ch-2 sp and last st, turn. Fasten off.

Row 11: With next color, rep row 10.

Row 12: With next color, rep row 10.

Row 13: Join first color in first st, ch 1, sc dec in first st and next ch-1 sp, *ch 2, sc in next ch-1 sp, ch 2, (sc, ch 2, sc) in next ch-2 sp, ch 2, sc in next ch-1 sp**, ch 2, dec in next 2 ch-1 sps, rep from * across, ending last rep at **, ch 2, sc dec in last ch-1 sp and last st, turn.

Rep rows 2–13 consecutively for pattern, ending with row 8. ■

Crested Waves

PATTERN NOTES
This uses 1 color.

Chain-3 at beginning of row or round counts as first double crochet unless otherwise stated.

SPECIAL STITCHES
V-stitch (V-st): (Dc, ch 1, dc) as indicated in instructions.

Shell: (Dc, {ch 1, dc} 4 times) as indicated in instructions.

INSTRUCTIONS
Row 1 (RS): Ch a multiple of 14 plus 18, dc in 4th ch from hook *dc in each of next 3 chs, sk next 3 chs, **V-st** (*see Special Stitches*) in next ch, sk next 3 sts, dc in each of next 3 chs**, 3 dc in next ch, rep from * across, ending last rep at **, 2 dc in last ch, turn.

Row 2 (WS): **Ch 3** (*see Pattern Notes*), dc in same st, sk next dc, ***fpdc** (*see Stitch Guide*) around each of next 3 sts, **shell** (*see Special Stitches*) in ch sp of next V-st, sk next 2 sts, fpdc around each of next 3 dc**, 3 dc in next dc, rep from * across, ending last rep at **, 2 dc in last st, turn.

Row 3: Ch 3, dc in same st, *dc in each of next 3 sts, V-st in center dc of next shell, sk next 3 dc, dc in each of next 3 sts, 3 dc in next st, rep from * across to last 2 sts, sk next st, 2 dc in last st, turn.

Rep rows 2 and 3 alternately for pattern. ■

Coastal Waves

PATTERN NOTES
This uses 2 colors.

Chain-3 at beginning of row or round counts as first double crochet unless otherwise stated.

Chain-4 at beginning of row or round counts as first double crochet and chain-1 unless otherwise stated.

SPECIAL STITCH
Cluster (cl): Holding back last lp of each st on hook, 2 dc as indicated in instructions, yo, pull through all lps on hook.

INSTRUCTIONS
Row 1 (RS): With first color, ch a multiple of 12 plus 13, sc in 2nd ch from hook and in each ch across, turn.

Row 2: Ch 1, sc in first st, ch 3, sk next 2 sts, *sc in next st, sk next 2 sts, 7 dc in next st, sk next 2 sts, sc in next st**, ch 7, sk next 5 sts, rep from * across, ending last rep at **, ch 3, sk next 2 sts, sc in last st, turn.

Row 3: Ch 1, sc in first st, *cl *(see Special Stitch)* in next dc, [ch 1, cl in next dc] 6 times**, working over ch-7 sp, sc in 3rd sk st, rep from * across, ending last rep at **, sc in last st, **changing color** *(see Stitch Guide)* to 2nd color in last st, turn.

Row 4: Ch 3 *(see Pattern Notes)*, 3 dc in same st, *sk next cl, sc in next cl, ch 7, sk next 3 cls**, sc in next cl, sk next cl, 7 dc in next sc, rep from * across, ending last rep at **, 4 dc in last st, turn.

Row 5: Ch 4 *(see Pattern Notes)*, cl in next dc, [ch 1, cl in next dc] twice, *working over ch-7, sc in 2nd sk cl of next cl group**, cl in next dc, [ch 1, cl in next dc] 6 times rep from * across, ending last rep at **, cl in next dc, [ch 1, cl in next dc] twice, ch 1, dc in last st, changing to first color in last st, turn.

Row 6: Ch 1, sc in first st, ch 3, sk next cl, sc in next cl, *7 dc in next sc, sk next cl, sc in next cl**, ch 7, sk next 3 cls, sc in next cl, sk next cl, rep from * across, ending last rep at **, ch 4, sk next cl, sc in last st, turn.

Row 7: Ch 1, sc in first st, *cl in next dc, [ch 1, cl in next dc] 6 times**, working over ch-7, sc in 2nd sk cl of next cl group, rep from * across, ending last rep at **, sc in last st, changing to 2nd color in last st, turn.

Rep rows 4–7 consecutively for pattern. ∎

Hopscotch

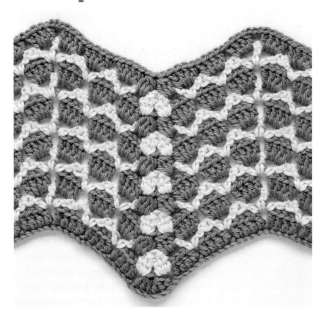

PATTERN NOTES

This uses 2 colors.

Join with slip stitch as indicated unless otherwise stated.

Chain-3 at beginning of row or round counts as first double crochet unless otherwise stated.

SPECIAL STITCHES

V-stitch (V-st): (Dc, ch 3, dc) as indicated in instructions.

Cluster (cl): Holding back last lp of each st on hook, 3 dc as indicated in instructions, yo, pull through all lps on hook.

INSTRUCTIONS

Row 1 (RS): With first color, ch a multiple of 36 plus 44, dc in 6th ch from hook, dc in each of next 3 chs, *[ch 1, sk next ch, dc in each of next 4 chs] 3 times, ch 3, [dc in each of next 4 chs, ch 1, sk next ch] 3 times**, [**dc dec** (see Stitch Guide) in next 3 chs] twice, rep from * across, ending last rep at **, dc in each of last 5 chs, turn. Fasten off.

Row 2: **Join** (see Pattern Notes) 2nd color in first st, **ch 3** (see Pattern Notes), [sk next dc group, **V-st** (see Special Stitches) in next ch-1 sp] 3 times, *(dc, {ch 1, dc} twice) in next ch-3 sp, [sk next dc group, V-st in next ch-1 sp] twice**, **cl** (see Special Stitches) in each of next 2 ch-1 sps, [sk next dc group, V-st in next ch-1 sp] twice, rep from * across, ending last rep at **, sk next dc group, V-st in next ch-1 sp, dc in last st, turn. Fasten off.

Row 3: Join first color in first st, ch 3, [4 dc in ch sp of next V-st, ch 1] twice, 4 dc in ch sp of next V-st, ch 3, 4 dc in next ch-1 sp, *[4 dc in ch sp of next V-st, ch 1] 3 times**, cl in next sp before next cl, cl in next sp after last cl, [ch 1, 4 dc in ch sp of next V-st] 3 times, rep from * across, ending last rep at **, 4 dc in ch sp of next V-st, dc in last st, turn. Fasten off.

Rep rows 2 and 3 alternately for pattern. ∎

Standout Chevron

PATTERN NOTES
This uses 3 colors.

Join with slip stitch as indicated unless otherwise stated.

SPECIAL STITCHES
Decrease (dec): Insert hook in next st, yo, pull lp through, yo 3 times, fpdtr around sc dec 5 rows below, [yo, pull through 2 lps on hook] 3 times, sk st on this row behind fpdtr, insert hook in next st, yo, pull lp through, yo, pull through all lps on hook.

Increase (inc): (Sc, fpdtr around same sc 5 rows below, sc) in next st.

INSTRUCTIONS
Row 1 (RS): With first color, ch a multiple of 18 plus 16, sc in 2nd ch from hook, sc in each of next 6 chs, *3 sc in next ch, sc in each of next 7 chs**, **sc dec** (see Stitch Guide) in next 3 chs, sc in each of next 7 chs, rep from * across, ending last rep at **, turn.

Row 2: Ch 1, sc dec in first 2 sts, sc in each of next 6 sts, *3 sc in next st**, sc in each of next 7 sts, sc dec in next 3 sts, sc in each of next 7 sts, rep from * across, ending last rep at **, sc in each of next 6 sts, sc dec in last 2 sts, turn. Fasten off.

Row 3: **Join** (see Pattern Notes) next color in first st, sc dec in same st and next st, sc in each of next 6 sts, *3 sc in next st**, sc in each of next 7 sts, sc dec in next 3 sts, sc in each of next 7 sts, rep from * across, ending last rep at **, sc in each of next 6 sts, sc dec in last 2 sts, turn.

Row 4: Ch 1, sc dec in first 2 sts, sc in each of next 6 sts, *3 sc in next st**, sc in each of next 7 sts, sc dec in next 3 sts, sc in each of next 7 sts, rep from * across, ending last rep at **, sc in each of next 6 sts, sc dec in last 2 sts, turn. Fasten off.

Row 5: Join next color in first st, sc dec in same st and next st, sc in each of next 6 sts, *3 sc in next st**, sc in each of next 7 sts, sc dec in next 3 sts, sc in each of next 7 sts, rep from * across, ending last rep at **, sc in each of next 6 sts, sc dec in last 2 sts, turn.

Row 6: Ch 1, sc dec in first 2 sts, sc in each of next 6 sts, *3 sc in next st**, sc in each of next 7 sts, sc dec in next 3 sts, sc in each of next 7 sts, rep from * across, ending last rep at **, sc in each of next 6 sts, sc dec in last 2 sts, turn. Fasten off.

Row 7: Join first color in first st, sc dec in same st and next st, sc in each of next 3 sts, **fpdtr** (see Stitch Guide) around center sc of sc group 5 rows below, sk next st on this row behind fpdtr, sc in each of next 2 sts, **inc** (see Special Stitches), sk next st on this row behind fpdtr inc, sc in each of next 2 sc, fpdtr around same sc as last fpdtr, sk next st on this row behind fpdtr, sc in each of next 4 sts, ***dec** (see Special Stitches), sk next st on this row behind dec, sc in each of next 4 sts, fpdtr around center sc of sc group 5 rows below, sk next st on this row behind fpdtr, sc in each of next 2 sts, fpdtr inc, sk next st on this row behind fpdtr inc, sc in each of next 2 sts, fpdtr around same center sc of sc group as last fpdtr, sk next st on this row behind fpdtr**, sc in each of next 4 sts, rep from * across, ending last rep at **, sc in each of next 3 sts, sc dec in last 2 sts, turn.

Rep rows 2–7 consecutively for pattern, ending with row 2. ∎

Northern Lights

PATTERN NOTES
This uses 3 colors.

Chain-2 at beginning of row or round **does not** count as first stitch unless otherwise stated.

Join with slip stitch as indicated unless otherwise stated.

SPECIAL STITCH
Decrease (dec): Holding back last lp of each st on hook, dc in next st, sk next 2 sts, dc in next st, yo, pull through all lps on hook.

INSTRUCTIONS
Row 1 (RS): With first color, ch a multiple of 42 plus 44, 3 dc in 5th ch from hook (*first 4 chs count as first dc, sk ch*), *[sk next 2 chs, dc in next ch, sk next 2 chs, 3 dc in next ch] twice, sk next 2 chs, dc in next ch, sk next 2 chs, (3 dc, ch 3, 3 dc) in next ch, [sk next 2 chs, dc in next ch, sk next 2 chs, 3 dc in next ch] 3 times**, sk next 2 chs, **dc dec** (*see Stitch Guide*) in next 3 chs, sk next 2 chs, 3 dc in next ch, rep from * across, ending last rep at **, sk next ch, dc in last ch, turn.

Row 2: Ch 1, sc in each st across with 3 sc in each ch-3 sp, turn. Fasten off.

Row 3: Join (*see Pattern Notes*) next color in first st, **ch 2** (*see Pattern Notes*), dc dec in next 2 sts, *[3 **fpdc** (*see Stitch Guide*) around next dc below, sk next 3 sts on this row, dc in next st] 3 times, (3 dc, ch 3, 3 dc) in next ch-3 sp, sk next 2 sts, dc in next st, 3 fpdc around next dc below, [sk next 3 sts, dc in next st, 3 fpdc around next dc below] twice**, sk next 3 sts, **dec** (*see Special Stitch*), rep from * across, ending last rep at **, dc dec in last 3 sts, turn. Fasten off.

Rep rows 2 and 3 alternately for pattern, working 2 rows of each color. ∎

Gentle Swells

PATTERN NOTES
This uses 1 color.

Chain-3 at beginning of row or round counts as first double crochet unless otherwise stated.

Chain-4 at beginning of row or round counts as first treble crochet unless otherwise stated.

Chain-5 at beginning of row or round counts as first double treble crochet unless otherwise stated.

INSTRUCTIONS
Row 1 (RS): Ch a multiple of 38 plus 21, dc in 4th ch from hook (*first 3 chs count as first dc*), dc in each ch across, turn.

Row 2: Ch 1, sc in first st, **fpsc** (*see Stitch Guide*) around each st across, ending with sc in last st, turn.

Row 3: Ch 4 (*see Pattern Notes*), 4 dtr in same st, *tr in next st, [sk next st, tr in next st] 8 times**, 5 dtr in each of next 2 sts, tr in next st, [sk next st, dtr in next st] 8 times, 5 dtr in each of next 2 sts, rep from * across, ending last rep at **, 5 dtr in last st, turn.

Row 4: Rep row 2.

Row 5: Ch 3 (*see Pattern Notes*), 5 dc in same st, *dc in next st, [sk next st, dc in next st] 8 times**, 5 dc in each of next 2 sts, dc in next st, [sk next st, dc in next st] 8 times, 5 dc in each of next 2 sts, rep from * across, ending last rep at **, 5 dc in last st, turn.

Row 6: Rep row 2.

Row 7: Ch 5 (*see Pattern Notes*), dtr in each st across, turn.

Rep rows 2–7 consecutively for pattern, ending with row 3. ∎

Waverly

PATTERN NOTES
This uses 3 colors.

Chain-2 at beginning of row or round **does not** count as first stitch unless otherwise stated.

Chain-1 spaces are counted as stitches when working across rows.

Join with slip stitch as indicated unless otherwise stated.

SPECIAL STITCHES

Decrease (dec): Holding back last lp of each st on hook, sk next ch, dc in next ch or st, sk next 2 chs or next dec, dc in next ch or st, yo, pull through all lps on hook.

Simple decrease (simple dec): Holding back last lp of each st on hook, dc in next st, sk next st, dc in next st, yo, pull through all lps on hook.

Back post double crochet decrease (bpdc dec): Holding back last lp of each st on hook, bpdc around next st, sk next dc or next dec, bpdc around next st, yo, pull through all lps on hook.

INSTRUCTIONS

Row 1 (RS): With first color, ch a multiple of 13 plus 15, dc in 5th ch from hook (*counts as first dc, ch-1 and sk 1 ch*), ch 1, sk next ch, dc in next ch, ch 1, sk next ch, *3 dc in next ch, ch 1, [sk next ch, dc in next ch, ch 1] twice**, **dec** (*see Special Stitches*), [ch 1, sk next ch, dc in next ch] twice, ch 1, rep from * across, ending last rep at **, sk next ch, dc in last ch, turn.

Row 2: **Ch 2** (*see Pattern Notes*), dc in next ch sp, [dc in next st, dc in next ch sp] twice, dc in next st *3 dc in next st, [dc in next st, dc in next ch sp] twice, dc in next dc**, **simple dec** (*see Special Stitches*) in next 2 ch sps, [dc in next st, dc in next ch sp] twice, dc in next dc, rep from * across, ending last rep at **, **dc dec** (*see Stitch Guide*) in last ch sp and last st, turn.

Row 3: Ch 2, dc in next st, [**fpdc** (*see Stitch Guide*) around next st, [**bpdc** (*see Stitch Guide*) around next st] twice, fpdc around next st, *3 dc in next dc, [fpdc around next dc, bpdc around next dc] twice, fpdc around next dc**, **bpdc dec** (*see Special Stitches*), [fpdc around next dc, bpdc around next dc] twice, fpdc around next dc, rep from * across, ending last rep at **, dc dec in last 2 sts, turn.

Row 4: Ch 2, dc in next st, fpdc around next st, [bpdc around next st, fpdc around next st] twice, *3 dc in next dc, [fpdc around next st, bpdc around next st] twice, fpdc around next st**, bpdc dec , [fpdc around next st, bpdc around next st] twice, fpdc around next st, rep from * across, ending last rep at **, dc dec in last 2 sts, turn.

Row 5: Ch 2, dc in next st, [ch 1, sk next st, dc in next st] twice, ch 1, sk next st, *3 dc in next st, [ch 1, sk next st, dc in next st] twice, ch 1**, dec, [ch 1, sk next st, dc in next st] twice, ch 1, sk next dc, rep from * across, ending last rep at **, sk next st, dc dec in last 2 sts, turn. Fasten off.

Row 6: Join next color with sc in first st, tr in each ch sp and sc in each st across, turn. Fasten off.

Row 7: **Join** (*see Pattern Notes*) next color in first st, ch 2, dc in next st, *dc in each of next 5 sts, 3 dc in next st, dc in each of next 5 sts**, simple dec, rep from * across, ending last rep at **, dc dec in last 2 sts, turn. Fasten off.

Row 8: Join 2nd color in first st, [tr in next st, sc in next st] across, turn. Fasten off.

Row 9: Join first color in first st, ch 2, dc in next st, [ch 1, sk next st, dc in next st] twice, ch 1, sk next st, *3 dc in next st, [ch 1, sk next st, dc in next st] twice, ch 1**, dec, [ch 1, sk next st, dc in next st] twice, ch 1, sk next dc, rep from * across, ending last rep at **, sk next st, dc dec in last 2 sts, turn.

Rep rows 2–9 consecutively for pattern, ending with row 5 or row 8. ■

Frothy Waters

PATTERN NOTES
This uses 3 colors.

Join with slip stitch as indicated unless otherwise stated.

Chain-4 at beginning of row or round counts as first double crochet and chain-1 unless otherwise stated.

SPECIAL STITCH
Popcorn (pc): 4 dc as indicated in instructions, drop lp from hook, insert hook from back to front through first dc of group, pull dropped lp through.

INSTRUCTIONS
Row 1 (RS): With first color, ch a multiple of 18 plus 16, sc in 2nd ch from hook, sc in each of next 2 chs, *ch 4, sk next 4 chs, (dc, {ch 1, dc} 6 times) in next ch**, ch 4, sk next 4 chs, sc in each of next 5 chs, rep from * across, ending last rep at **, ch 2, sk next 4 chs, sc in each of last 3 chs, turn.

Row 2: **Ch 4** (*see Pattern Notes*), (dc, {ch 1, dc} twice) in same st, *[ch 2, **pc** (*see Special Stitch*) in next ch-1 sp] 6 times, ch 2, sk next sc**, sc in each of next 3 sc, rep from * across, ending last rep at **, sc in each of last 2 sts, turn. Fasten off.

Row 3: **Join** (*see Pattern Notes*) next color in first st, ch 4, (dc, {ch 1, dc} twice) in same st, *ch 2, sk next 2 ch-2 sps, sc in next ch-2 sp, [sc in next pc, sc in next ch-2 sp] twice**, ch 2, sk next sc, (dc, {ch 1, dc} 6 times) in next sc, rep from * across, ending last rep at **, ch 2, (dc, {ch 1, dc} twice) in last st, turn.

Row 4: Ch 4, [pc in next ch-1 sp, ch 2] 3 times, *sk next sc, sc in each of next 3 sc, ch 2*, [pc in next ch-1 sp, ch 2] 6 times, rep from * across, ending last rep at **, [pc in next ch-1 sp, ch 2] twice, pc in last ch-1 sp, ch 1, dc in last st, turn. Fasten off.

Row 5: Join next color with sc in first st, sc in each of next 2 sts, *ch 4, sk next sc, (dc, {ch 1, dc} 6 times) in next sc, ch 4, sk next 2 ch-2 sps**, sc in next ch-2 sp, [sc in next pc, sc in next ch-2 sp] twice, rep from * across, ending last rep at **, sc in next ch-2 sp, sc in next pc, sc in last st, turn.

Rep rows 2–5 consecutively for pattern, ending with row 2. ∎

Bubbles

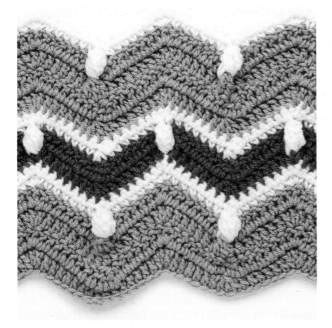

PATTERN NOTES
This uses 3 colors.

Join with slip stitch as indicated unless otherwise stated.

Chain-2 at beginning of row or round counts as first double crochet unless otherwise stated.

SPECIAL STITCH
Popcorn (pc): 5 fpdc (*see Stitch Guide*) around st as indicated in instructions, drop lp from hook, insert hook in first fpdc of group, pull dropped lp through, ch 1 to close.

INSTRUCTIONS
Row 1 (RS): With first color, ch a multiple of 16 plus 18, dc in 3rd ch from hook (*first 2 chs count as first dc*), *dc in each of next 6 chs, 3 dc in next ch, dc in each of next 6 chs**, **dc dec** (*see Stitch Guide*) in next 3 chs, rep from * across, ending last rep at **, dc dec in last 2 chs, turn.

Rows 2–4: **Ch 2** (*see Pattern Notes*), dc in next dc, *dc in each of next 6 dc, 3 dc in next dc, dc in each of next 6 dc**, dc dec in next 3 dc, rep from * across, ending last rep at **, dc dec in last 2 dc, turn. Fasten off.

Row 5: **Join** (*see Pattern Notes*) next color in first st, ch 1, **sc dec** (*see Stitch Guide*) in same st and next st, *sc in each of next 6 dc, 3 sc in next dc, sc in each of next 6 dc**, sk next dc, **pc** (*see Special Stitch*) around dc dec 2 rows below, sk next dc on this row, rep from * across, ending last rep at **, sc dec in last 2 dc, turn.

Row 6: Ch 1, sc dec in first 2 sc, *sc in each of next 6 sc, 3 sc in next sc, sc in each of next 6 sc**, sc dec in next 3 sc, rep from * across, ending last rep at **, dc dec in last 2 sts, turn. Fasten off.

Row 7: Join next color in first st, ch 2, dc in next sc, *dc in each of next 6 sc, 3 dc in next sc, dc in each of next 6 sc**, dc dec in next 3 sts, rep from * across, ending last rep at **, dc dec in last 2 sc, turn.

Row 8: Ch 2, dc in next st, *dc in each of next 6 dc, 3 dc in next dc, dc in each of next 6 dc**, dc dec in next 3 dc, rep from * across, ending last rep at **, dc dec in last 2 dc, turn. Fasten off.

Row 9: Join 2nd color in first st, sc dec in same st and next st, *sc in each of next 6 dc, (sc, pc around center dc 2 rows below, sc) in next dc, sc in each of next 6 dc**, sk next dc, sc dec in next 3 dc, rep from * across, ending last rep at **, sc dec in last 2 dc, turn.

Row 10: Ch 1, sc dec in first 2 sc, *sc in each of next 6 sc, 3 sc in next sc, sc in each of next 6 sc**, sc dec in next 3 sc, rep from * across, ending last rep at **, sc dec in last 2 sc, turn. Fasten off.

Row 11: Join first color in first sc, ch 2, dc in next sc, *dc in each of next 6 sc, 3 dc in next sc, dc in each of next 6 sc**, dc dec in next 3 sc, rep from * across, ending last rep at **, dc dec in last 2 sc, turn.

Rep rows 2–11 consecutively for pattern, ending with row 6. ■

Double Wrap

PATTERN NOTES
This uses 1 color.

Chain-3 at beginning of row or round counts as
first double crochet unless otherwise stated.

SPECIAL STITCHES
Cluster (cl): Holding back last lp of each st on
hook, 2 dc around **post** (*see Stitch Guide*) of last
2 dc worked, yo, pull through all lps on hook.

Wrap: 2 dc as indicated in instructions,
cl around post of both dc just made.

INSTRUCTIONS
Row 1 (RS): Ch a multiple of 41 plus 42, dc in
4th ch from hook, dc in next ch, **cl** (*see Special
Stitches*), [sk next 2 chs, **wrap** (*see Special
Stitches*) in next 2 chs] 4 times, *ch 3, wrap in
next 2 chs, [sk next 2 chs, wrap in next 2 chs]
4 times, sk next 2 chs, dc in next ch**, [sk next
2 chs, wrap in next 2 chs] 5 times, rep from *
across, ending last rep at **, turn.

Row 2: Ch 3 (*see Pattern Notes*), sk wrap, *[wrap
in sp between last wrap and next wrap] 4 times,
(wrap, ch 3, wrap) in next ch-3 sp, [wrap in sp
between last wrap and next wrap] 4 times, sk
next wrap, dc in next dc, rep from * across, turn.

Rep row 2 for pattern. ∎

Raised Ripples

PATTERN NOTE
This uses 3 colors.

INSTRUCTIONS (116)
Row 1 (RS): With first color, ch a multiple of 10
plus 6, sc in 2nd ch from hook and in each ch
across, turn. (114)

Rows 2–4: Ch 1, sc in each st across. At end of
last row, fasten off.

Row 5: Join next color with sc in first st, sc in
each of next 4 sts, *fphdc (*see Stitch Guide*)
around next sc 2 rows below, **fpdc** (*see Stitch
Guide*) around each of next 3 sts 3 rows below,

fphdc around next sc 2 rows below, sc in each of next 5 sts on this row, rep from * across, turn.

Rep rows 2–5 consecutively for pattern, working 4 rows with each color. ∎

Infusion

PATTERN NOTES
This uses 1 color.

Chain-3 at beginning of row or round counts as first double crochet unless otherwise stated.

Chain-4 at beginning of row or round counts as first double crochet and chain-1 unless otherwise stated.

SPECIAL STITCHES
V-stitch (V-st): (Dc, ch 1, dc) as indicated in instructions.

Cluster (cl): Holding back last lp of each st on hook, 2 dc as indicated in instructions, yo, pull through all lps on hook.

Cluster decrease (cl dec): Holding back last lp of each st on hook, 2 dc in next st, sk next dec, 2 dc in next st, yo, pull through all lps on hook.

Decrease (dec): Holding back last lp of each st on hook, dc as in next ch or st, sk next ch or st, dc in next ch or st, yo, pull through all lps on hook.

INSTRUCTIONS
Row 1 (RS): Ch a multiple of 14 plus 18, dc in 4th ch from hook, *dc in each of next 5 chs, **dec** *(see Special Stitches)*, dc in each of next 5 chs**, **V-st** *(see Special Stitches)* in next ch, rep from * across, ending last rep at **, 2 dc in last ch, turn.

Row 2: Ch 3 *(see Pattern Notes)*, dc in same st, *dc in each of next 5 sts, dec, dc in each of next 5 sts**, V-st in ch sp of next V-st, rep from * across, ending last rep at **, 2 dc in last st, turn.

Row 3: Ch 4 *(see Pattern Notes)*, **cl** *(see Special Stitches)* in same st, *ch 2, sk next 2 sts, cl in next st, ch 2, sk next 2 sts, **cl dec** *(see Special Stitches)*, ch 2, sk next 2 sts, cl, ch 2, sk next 2 sts**, (cl, ch 4, cl) in ch sp of next V-st, rep from * across, ending last rep at **, (cl, ch 1, dc) in last st, turn.

Row 4: Ch 1, sc in first st, 2 sc in next ch-1 sp, *2 sc in each of next 2 ch-2 sps, sc in top of next cl dec, 2 sc in each of next 2 ch-2 sps**, 5 sc in next ch-4 sp, rep from * across, ending last rep at **, 2 sc in last ch-1 sp, sc in last st, turn.

Row 5: Ch 3, dc in same st, *dc in each of next 5 sts, dec, dc in each of next 5 sts**, V-st in next st, rep from * across, ending last rep at **, 2 dc in last st, turn.

Rep rows 2–5 consecutively for pattern, ending with row 3. ∎

Violets

PATTERN NOTES
This uses 3 colors.

Join with slip stitch as indicated unless otherwise stated.

Chain-3 at beginning of row or round counts as first double crochet unless otherwise stated.

SPECIAL STITCHES
Cluster (cl): Holding back last lp of each st on hook, 2 dc as indicated in instructions, yo, pull through all lps on hook.

Leaf: Ch 5, sl st in 2nd ch from hook, sc in next ch, hdc in next ch, dc in next ch.

Violet: [Ch 4, sl st in 4th ch from hook] 5 times, turning as you work.

INSTRUCTIONS
Row 1 (RS): With first color, ch a multiple of 27 plus 32, dc in 6th ch from hook, dc in next ch, [ch 1, sk next ch, dc in each of next 2 chs] 3 times, ch 1, sk next ch, *(2 dc, ch 3, 2 dc) in next ch, [ch 1, sk next ch, dc in each of next 2 chs] 3 times, ch 1, sk next ch**, **dc dec** (*see Stitch Guide*) in next 2 chs, sk next 2 chs, dc dec in next 2 chs, [ch 1, sk next ch, dc in each of next 2 chs] 3 times, ch 1, sk next ch, rep from * across, ending last rep at **, dc in each of next 2 chs, sk next ch, dc in last ch, turn.

Row 2: Ch 3 (*see Pattern Notes*), 2 dc in each of next 4 ch-1 sps, *(2 dc, ch 3, 2 dc) in next ch-3 sp, 2 dc in each of next 3 ch-1 sps**, **cl** (*see Special Stitches*) in each of next 2 ch-1 sps, 2 dc in each of next 3 ch-1 sps, rep from * across, ending last rep at **, 2 dc in next ch-1 sp, dc in last st, turn.

Rows 3–5: Ch 3, sk next 2 sts, working in sps between dc groups, 2 dc in each of next 4 sps, *(2 dc, ch 3, 2 dc) in next ch-3 sp, 2 dc in each of next 3 sps**, cl in next sp, sk next 2 cls, cl in next sp, 2 dc in each of next 3 sps, rep from * across, ending last rep at **, 2 dc in next sp, dc in last st, turn. At end of last row, fasten off.

Row 6: With WS facing, join next color with sc in first st, sc in each of next 4 sts, **leaf** (*see Special Stitches*), sc in each of next 5 sts, leaf, sc in next st, *3 sc in next ch-3 sp, sc in next st, leaf, sc in each of next 5 sts, leaf**, sc in each of next 2 sts, **sc dec** (*see Stitch Guide*) in next 2 sts, sc in each of next 2 sts, leaf, sc in each of next 5 sts, leaf, sc in next st, rep from * across, ending last rep at **, sc in each of last 5 sts, turn. Fasten off.

Row 7: With RS facing, join next color with sc in first st, sc in each of next 2 sts, *violet (*see Special Stitches*), holding leaves to front of work, sc in each of next 5 sts, rep from * across to last 2 sts, violet, sc in each of last 2 sts, turn.

Row 8: Ch 1, sc in each st across, turn. Fasten off.

Row 9: With RS facing, **join** *(see Pattern Notes)* first color in first st, ch 3, sk next 3 sts, [2 dc in next st, ch 1, sk next st] 4 times, *(2 dc, ch 3, 2 dc) in next st, [ch 1, sk next st, 2 dc in next st] 3 times, sk next st**, cl in next st, sk next 3 sts, cl in next st, [ch 1, sk next st, 2 dc in next st] 3 times, ch 1, sk next st, rep from * across, ending last rep at **, 2 dc in next st, dc in last st, turn.

Rep rows 2–9 consecutively for pattern, ending with row 5. ■

Lyrical

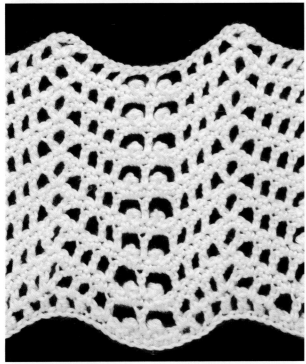

PATTERN NOTES
This uses 1 color.

Chain-5 at beginning of row or round counts as first double crochet and chain-2 unless otherwise stated.

SPECIAL STITCH
Picot: Ch 3, sl st in 3rd ch from hook.

INSTRUCTIONS
Row 1 (RS): Ch a multiple of 20 plus 12, sc in 2nd ch from hook, sc in next ch, **picot** *(see Special Stitch)*, sc in each of next 2 chs, ch 1, sk next ch, sc in next ch, ch 1, sk next ch, hdc in next ch, ch 1, sk next ch, [dc in next ch, ch 1, sk next ch] 3 times, hdc in next ch, ch 1, sk next ch, sc in each of next 3 chs, picot, sc in next ch, rep from * across, turn.

Row 2: Ch 5 *(see Pattern Notes)*, dc in 4th sc, *ch 1, [dc in next ch-1 sp, ch 1] twice, sk next ch-1 sp, (dc, ch 3, dc) in next dc, sk next ch-1 sp**, [ch 1, dc in next ch-1 sp] 3 times, ch 2, dc in sc between next 2 picots, ch 2, dc in next ch-1 sp, rep from * across, ending last rep at **, [ch 1, dc in next ch-1 sp] twice, ch 1, dc in next sc, ch 2, dc in last st, turn.

Row 3: Ch 1, sc in first st, *(sc, picot, sc) in next ch-2 sp, [sc in next dc, sc in next ch-1 sp] 3 times, sc in next dc, 3 sc in next ch-3 sp, sc in next dc, [sc in next ch-1 sp, sc in next dc] 3 times, (sc, picot, sc) in next ch-2 sp, sc in next dc, rep from * across, turn.

Row 4: Ch 5, dc in 5th sc, *[ch 1, sk next sc, dc in next sc] twice, ch 1, sk next 2 sc, (dc, ch 3, dc) in next sc, ch 1, sk next 2 sc, [dc in next sc, ch 1, sk next sc] twice, dc in next sc, ch 2, sk next 3 sc**, dc in next sc between picots, ch 2, sk next 3 sc, dc in next sc, rep from * across, ending last rep at **, dc in last st, turn.

Rep rows 3 and 4 alternately for pattern. ■

Accent

PATTERN NOTES

This uses 1 color.

Chain-4 at beginning of row or round counts as first double crochet and chain-1 unless otherwise stated.

INSTRUCTIONS

Row 1 (RS): Ch a multiple of 20 plus 24, 2 dc in 5th ch from hook (*first 4 chs count as first dc and ch-1*), *[ch 1, sk next ch, dc in next ch] 3 times, sk next 2 chs, dc in each of next 2 chs, sk next 2 chs, [dc in next ch, ch 1, sk next ch] 3 times**, 2 dc in next ch, ch 2, 2 dc in next ch, rep from * across, ending last rep at **, (2 dc, ch 1, dc) in last ch, turn.

Row 2: Ch 4 (*see Pattern Notes*), 2 dc in next ch-1 sp, *sk next dc, [ch 1, dc in next dc] 3 times, sk next dc, **bpdc** (*see Stitch Guide*) around each of next 2 dc, sk next dc, [dc in next dc, ch 1] 3 times**, (2 dc, ch 2, 2 dc) in next ch-2 sp, rep from * across, ending last rep at **, sk next dc, (2 dc, ch 1, dc) in last ch-1 sp, turn.

Row 3: Ch 4, 2 dc in first ch-1 sp, *sk next dc, [ch 1, dc in next dc] 3 times, sk next dc, **fpdc** (*see Stitch Guide*) around each of next 2 bpdc, sk next dc, [dc in next dc, ch 1] 3 times**, (2 dc, ch 2, 2 dc) in next ch-2 sp, rep from * across, ending last rep at **, (2 dc, ch 1, dc) in last ch-1 sp, turn.

Rep rows 2 and 3 alternately for pattern. ∎

Happy Times

PATTERN NOTES

This uses 4 colors.

Join with slip stitch as indicated unless otherwise stated.

Chain-3 at beginning of row or round counts as first double crochet unless otherwise stated.

Chain-2 at beginning of row or round counts as first half double crochet unless otherwise stated.

SPECIAL STITCHES

Cluster (cl): Holding back last lp of each st on hook, 3 dc as indicated in instructions, yo, pull through all lps on hook.

Corkscrew: Ch 12, 3 sc in 2nd ch from hook and in each ch across.

INSTRUCTIONS

Row 1 (RS): With first color, ch a multiple of 27 plus 23, 3 dc in 4th ch from hook (*first 3 chs count as first dc*), [sk next 2 chs, 3 dc in next ch] twice, sk next 2 chs, *(3 dc, ch 3, 3 dc) in next ch, sk next 2 chs, [3 dc in next ch, sk next 2 chs] twice**, **dc dec** (*see Stitch Guide*) in next 3 chs, sk next 4 chs, dc dec in next 3 chs, sk next 2 chs, [3 dc in next ch, sk next 2 chs] twice, rep from * across, ending last rep at **, 3 dc in next ch, dc in last ch, turn.

Row 2: Ch 3 (*see Pattern Notes*), [sk next 3 dc, 3 dc in sp before next dc] 3 times, sk next 3 dc, *(3 dc, ch 3, 3 dc) in next ch-3 sp, [sk next 3 dc, 3 dc in sp before next dc] twice**, **cl** (*see Special Stitches*) in sp before next dc dec, sk next 2 dc dec, cl in sp before next dc, [sk next 3 dc, 3 dc in sp before next dc] twice, rep from * across, ending last rep at **, sk next 3 dc, 3 dc in sp before next dc, dc in last st, turn.

Rows 3 & 4: Rep row 2. At end of last row, fasten off.

Row 5: Join (*see Pattern Notes*) next color in first st, **ch 2** (*see Pattern Notes*), **hdc dec** (*see Stitch Guide*) in next 3 sts, hdc in each of next 9 sts, *3 hdc in next ch-3 sp, hdc in each of next 8 sts**, [hdc dec in next 2 sts] twice, hdc in each of next 8 sts, rep from * across, ending last rep at **, hdc in next st, hdc dec in next 3 sts, hdc in last st, turn. Fasten off.

Row 6: Join first color in first st, ch 3, [sk next 2 sts, 3 dc in next st] 3 times, *sk next 2 sts, (3 dc, ch 3, 3 dc) in next st, sk next 2 sts, [3 dc in next st, sk next 2 sts] twice**, cl in each of next 2 sts, [sk next 2 sts, 3 dc in next st] twice, rep from * across, ending last rep at **, 3 dc in next st, dc in last st, turn. Fasten off.

Row 7: Join next color in first st, ch 2, hdc dec in next 3 sts, hdc in each of next 9 sts, *(hdc, **corkscrew**—*see Special Stitches*, hdc) in next ch-3 sp, hdc in each of next 8 sts**, hdc dec in next 2 sts, corkscrew, hdc dec in next 2 sts, hdc in each of next 8 sts, rep from * across, ending last rep at **, hdc in next st, hdc dec in next 3 sts, hdc in last st, turn. Fasten off.

Row 8: Join first color in first st, ch 3, 3 dc in next st, *[sk next 2 sts, 3 dc in next st] twice, sk next 2 sts, 3 dc in next st, ch 3, sk corkscrew, 3 dc in next st, [sk next 2 sts, 3 dc in next st] twice, sk next 2 sts**, cl in next st, sk corkscrew, cl in next st, rep from * across, ending last rep at **, 3 dc in next st, dc in last st, turn. Fasten off.

Row 9: With last color, rep row 5, **do not turn**. Fasten off.

Row 10: With RS facing, join first color in first st, ch 2, sk next st, [3 dc in next st, sk next 2 sts] 3 times, sk next 2 sts, *(3 dc, ch 3, 3 dc) in next st, [sk next 2 sts, 3 dc in next st] twice, sk next 2 sts**, [dc dec in next 2 sts] twice, [sk next 2 sts, 3 dc in next st] twice, sk next 2 sts, rep from * across, ending last rep at **, 3 dc in next st, dc in last st, turn.

Rows 11–13: Ch 3, [sk next 3 dc, 3 dc in sp before next dc] 3 times, sk next 3 dc, *(3 dc, ch 3, 3 dc) in next ch-3 sp, [sk next 3 dc, 3 dc in sp before next dc] twice**, cl in sp before next dc dec, sk next 2 dc dec, cl in sp before next dc, [sk next 3 dc, 3 dc in sp before next 3 dc] twice, rep from * across, ending last rep at **, 3 dc in sp before next dc, dc in last st, turn.

Rep rows 5–13 consecutively for pattern. ■

Gemstones

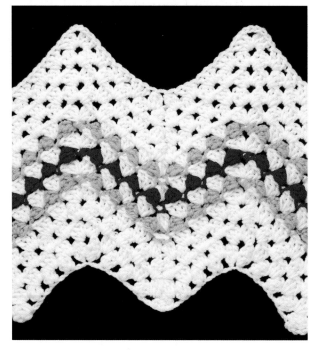

PATTERN NOTES

This uses 4 colors.

Chain-3 at beginning of row or round counts as first double crochet unless otherwise stated.

Join with slip stitch as indicated unless otherwise stated.

SPECIAL STITCHES

3-double crochet cluster (3-dc cl): Holding back last lp of each st on hook, 3 dc as indicated in instructions, yo, pull through all lps on hook.

2-double crochet cluster (2-dc cl): Ch 3, holding back last lp of each st on hook, 2 dc in 3rd ch from hook, yo, pull through all lps on hook.

INSTRUCTIONS

Row 1 (RS): With first color, ch a multiple of 26 plus 33, 3 dc in 6th ch from hook (*first 5 chs count as first dc and sk 2 chs*), *[sk next 2 chs, 3 dc in next ch] 3 times, sk next 2 chs, (3 dc, ch 3, 3 dc) in next ch, [sk next 2 chs, 3 dc in next ch] 3 times, sk next 2 chs**, **dc dec** (*see Stitch Guide*) in next 3 chs, rep from * across, ending last rep at **, 3 dc in next ch, sk next 2 chs, dc in last ch, turn.

Rows 2–4: Ch 3 (*see Pattern Notes*), sk next 3 sts, 3 dc in sp between last dc and next dc group, *[3 dc in sp between last dc group and next dc group] 3 times, (3 dc, ch 3, 3 dc) in next ch-3 sp, [dc in sp between last dc group and next dc group] 3 times, sk next dc group**, **3-dc cl** (*see Special Stitches*) in sp between last dc and first dc of next dc group, sk next dc dec, 3-dc cl in sp between last dc and first dc of next dc group, rep from * across, ending last rep at **, sk next dc group, 3 dc in sp between last dc and next dc group, dc in last st, turn. At end of last row, fasten off.

Row 5: With RS facing, join next color with sc in first st, **2-dc cl** (*see Special Stitches*), sk next dc group, [sc in sp between next dc group, 2-dc cl] 4 times**, 3 sc in next ch-3 sp, [cl, sc between next dc group] 3 times, **sc dec** (*see Stitch Guide*) in next 3 sps, [2-dc cl, sc in next sp between dc group] 3 times, 2-dc cl, rep from * across, ending last rep at **, sc in last st, turn. Fasten off.

Row 6: With RS facing, **join** (*see Pattern Notes*) first color in first st, ch 3, 3 dc in each of next 4 sps, *(3 dc, ch 3, 3 dc) in 2nd sc of next sc group, 3 dc in each of next 3 sc**, 3-dc cl in next dec, 3 dc in each of next 3 sc, rep from * across, ending last rep at **, 3 dc in next sc, dc in last st, turn. Fasten off.

Row 7: Join next color with sc in first st, cl, sk next dc group, [sc in next sp between dc group, 2-dc cl] 4 times, *3 sc in next ch-3 sp, [2-dc cl, sc in next sp between dc group] 3 times, 2-dc cl**, sc dec in sps on each side of next dec, rep from * across, ending last rep at **, sc in next sp between dc group, 2-dc cl, sc in last st, turn. Fasten off.

Row 8: With first color, rep row 6.

Row 9: With last color, rep row 7.

Row 10: With first color, rep row 6, **do not fasten off** at end of row.

Rows 11–14: Ch 3, sk next 3 sts, 3 dc in next sp between dc group, *[3 dc in sp between dc group] 3 times, (3 dc, ch 3, 3 dc) in next ch-3 sp, [dc in next sp between next dc group] 3 times, sk next dc group**, [dc dec in next sp between dc group] twice, rep from * across, ending last rep at **, sk next dc group, 3 dc in next sp between next dc group, dc in last st, turn. At end of last row, fasten off.

Rep rows 5–14 consecutively for pattern, ending with row 13. ■

Pretty Posies

PATTERN NOTES
This uses 3 colors.

Join with slip stitch as indicated unless otherwise stated.

Chain-3 at beginning of row or round counts as first double crochet unless otherwise stated.

INSTRUCTIONS
Row 1 (RS): With first color, ch a multiple of 18 plus 21, dc in 4th ch from hook (*first 3 chs counts as first dc*), *dc in each of next 6 chs, sk next ch, dc in each of next 2 chs, sk next ch, dc in each of next 6 chs**, 2 dc in each of next 2 chs, rep from * across, ending last rep at **, 2 dc in last st, turn.

Row 2: Ch 3 (*see Pattern Notes*), dc in same st, *dc in each of next 6 sts, sk next st, **bpdc** (*see Stitch Guide*) around each of next 2 sts, sk next st, dc in each of next 6 sts**, 2 dc in each of next 2 sts, rep from * across, ending last rep at **, 2 dc in last st, turn. Fasten off.

Row 3: With RS facing, **join** (*see Pattern Notes*) next color in first st, ch 3, dc in same st, *dc in each of next 6 sts, sk next st, **fpdc** (*see Stitch Guide*) around each of next 2 sts, sk next st, dc in each of next 6 sts**, 2 dc in each of next 2 sts, rep from * across, ending last rep at **, 2 dc in last st, turn.

Row 4: Rep row 2.

Row 5: With RS facing, join next color in first st, ch 3, dc in same st, *dc in each of next 6 sts, sk next st, fpdc around each of next 2 sts, ch 1, (sl st, {ch 5, sl st} 3 times) around last fpdc worked, ch 5, (sl st, {ch 5, sl st} 3 times) around previous fpdc worked (*flower completed*), sk next st, dc in each of next 6 sts**, 2 dc in each of next 2 sts, rep from * across, ending last rep at **, 2 dc in last st, turn.

Row 6: Ch 3, dc in same st, dc in each of next 6 sts, *sk next st, 2 dc in center of flower, sk next st, dc in each of next 6 sts**, sk next st, 2 dc in each of next 2 sts, rep from * across, ending last rep at **, 2 dc in last st, turn. Fasten off.

Row 7: With RS facing, join first color in first st, ch 3, dc in same st, *dc in each of next 6 sts, sk next st, fpdc around each of next 2 sts, sk next st, dc in each of next 6 sts**, 2 dc in each of next 2 sts, rep from * across, ending last rep at **, 2 dc in last st, turn.

Rep rows 2–7 consecutively for pattern, ending with row 2. ■

Suspension

PATTERN NOTES
This uses 1 color.

Chain-2 at beginning of row or round **does not** count as first stitch unless otherwise stated.

SPECIAL STITCH
Cluster (cl): Holding back last lp of each st on hook, 3 dc as indicated in instructions, yo, pull through all lps on hook.

INSTRUCTIONS
Row 1 (RS): Ch a multiple of 32 plus 32, sc in 2nd ch from hook, *[ch 3, sk next 2 chs, sc in next ch] 4 times, ch 3, sk next 2 chs, (sc, ch 3, sc) in next ch, [ch 3, sk next 2 chs, sc in next ch] 4 times, ch 3, sk next 2 chs**, **sc dec** (see Stitch Guide) in next 3 chs, rep from * across, ending last rep at **, sc in last ch, turn.

Row 2: Ch 2 (see Pattern Notes), dc in next ch-3 sp, *[ch 1, 3 dc in next ch-3 sp, ch 1, **cl** (see Special Stitch) in next ch-3 sp] twice, ch 1, (3 dc, ch 3, 3 dc) in next ch-3 sp, [ch 1, cl in next ch-3 sp, ch 1, 3 dc in next ch-3 sp] twice**, ch 1, **dc dec** (see Stitch Guide) in next ch-3 sp, next sc dec and next ch-3 sp, rep from * across, ending last rep at **, dc dec in last ch-3 sp and last st, turn.

Row 3: Ch 1, sc in sp between last dc dec and next dc group, *[ch 3, sc in next ch-1 sp] 4 times, ch 3, (sc, ch 3, sc) in next ch-3 sp, [ch 3, sc in next ch-1 sp] 4 times**, ch 3, sc dec in next ch-1 sp, next dc dec and next ch-1 sp, rep from * across, ending last rep at **, ch 3, sc in last ch-1 sp, turn.

Rep rows 2 and 3 alternately for pattern, ending with row 2. ■

Mistletoe

PATTERN NOTES
This uses 3 colors.

Chain-3 at beginning of row or round counts as first double crochet unless otherwise stated.

SPECIAL STITCH
Popcorn (pc): 6 dc in sp between 2 dc dec below through center leaf, drop lp from hook, insert hook in first dc of group, pull dropped lp through, ch 1 to secure.

INSTRUCTIONS
Row 1 (WS): With first color, ch a multiple of 14 plus 17, 2 dc in 4th ch from hook (first 3 chs count as first dc), *dc in each of next 3 chs, [**dc dec** (see Stitch Guide) in next 3 chs] twice, dc in each of next 3 chs**, 3 dc in each of next 2 chs, rep from * across, ending last rep at **, 3 dc in last ch, turn.

Rows 2–6: Ch 3 (see Pattern Notes), 2 dc in same st, *dc in each of next 3 sts, [dc dec in next 3 sts] twice, dc in each of next 3 sts**, 3 dc in each of next 2 sts, rep from * across, ending last rep at **, 3 dc in last st, turn. At end of last row, fasten off.

Row 7: Join next color with sc in first st, dc in each of next 6 sts, *ch 6, sl st in 6th ch from hook, ch 9, sl st in same ch as last sl st, ch 6, sl st in same ch as last sl st (leaf group)**, sc in each of next 14 sts, rep from * across, ending last rep at **, sc in each of last 7 sts, turn. Fasten off.

Row 8: Join next color with sc in first st, sc in each of next 6 sts, ***pc** (see Special Stitch)**, sc in each of next 14 sts, rep from * across, ending last rep at **, sc in each of last 7 sts, turn. Fasten off.

Row 9: With RS facing, join first color in first st, ch 3, 2 dc in same st, *dc in each of next 3 sts, dc dec in next 3 sts, sk next pc, dc dec in next 3 sts, dc in each of next 3 sts**, 3 dc in each of next 2 sts, rep from * across, ending last rep at **, 3 dc in last st, turn.

Rep rows 2–9 consecutively for pattern, ending with row 8. ■

Little Hearts

PATTERN NOTES
This uses 2 colors.

Carry colors at ends of rows.

INSTRUCTIONS
Row 1 (RS): With first color, ch a multiple of 13 plus 12, sc in 2nd ch from hook, sc in each of next 4 chs, *3 sc in next ch, sc in each of next 5 chs**, sk next 2 chs, sc in each of next 5 chs, rep from * across, ending last rep at **, turn.

Row 2: Ch 1, **sc dec** (see Stitch Guide) in first 2 sts, sc in each of next 4 sts, *3 sc in next sc**, sc in each of next 5 sc, sk next 2 sc, sc in each of next 5 sc, rep from * across, ending last rep at **, sc in each of next 4 sts, sc dec in last 2 sts, **changing colors** (see Stitch Guide) to 2nd color in last st, turn. **Drop first color** (see Pattern Notes).

Row 3: Ch 1, sc dec in first 2 sts, sc in each of next 4 sts, *3 sc in next sc**, sc in each of next 5 sc, sk next 2 sc, sc in each of next 5 sc, rep from * across, ending last rep at **, sc in each of next 4 sts, sc dec in last 2 sts, turn.

Row 4: Rep row 2, changing to first color. Drop 2nd color.

Row 5: Ch 1, sc dec in first 2 sts, sc in next st, **fpdc** (see Stitch Guide) around first sc of sc group at peak 2 rows below, fpdc around 2nd sc of same sc group, sc in next st on this row, *3 sc in next sc, sc in next sc, fpdc around same st as last fpdc, fpdc around next sc on same row as last fpdc**, sc in each of next 2 sc, sk next 2 sc, sc in each of next 2 sc, fpdc around first sc of next sc group at peak 2 rows below, fpdc around 2nd sc of same group**, sc in next sc, rep from * across, ending last rep at **, sc in next sc, sc dec in last 2 sts, turn.

Row 6: Rep row 2.

Rep rows 3–6 consecutively for pattern. ■

Wee Ripples

PATTERN NOTES
This uses 2 colors.

Join with slip stitch as indicated unless otherwise stated.

INSTRUCTIONS
Row 1 (RS): With first color, ch a multiple of 7 plus 6, working in **back lps** (*see Stitch Guide*), sc in 2nd ch from hook, sc in next ch, *3 sc in next ch, sc in each of next 2 chs**, sk next 2 chs, sc in each of next 2 chs, rep from * across, ending last rep at **, turn.

Row 2: Working in back lps, ch 1, **sc dec** (*see Stitch Guide*) in first 2 sts, sc in next st, *3 sc in next st, sc in each of next 2 sts, sk next 2 sts, sc in each of next 2 sts, rep from * across to last 3 sts, sc in next st, sc dec in last 2 sts, turn. Fasten off.

Row 3: Working in back lps, **join** (*see Pattern Notes*) next color in first st, ch 1, sc dec in same st and next st, sc in next st, *3 sc in next st, sc in each of next 2 sts, sk next 2 sts, sc in each

of next 2 sts, rep from * across to last 3 sts, sc in next st, sc dec in last 2 sts, turn.

Row 4: Working in back lps, ch 1, sc dec in first 2 sts, sc in next st, *3 sc in next st, sc in each of next 2 sts, sk next 2 sts, sc in each of next 2 sts, rep from * across to last 3 sts, sc in next st, sc dec in last 2 sts, turn. Fasten off.

Rep rows 3 and 4 alternately for pattern, working 2 rows of each color. ■

Blissful

PATTERN NOTE
This uses 1 color.

SPECIAL STITCH
Puff stitch (puff st): [Yo, insert hook as indicated in instructions, yo, pull lp through] 4 times, yo, pull through all lps on hook.

INSTRUCTIONS
Row 1 (RS): Ch a multiple of 27 plus 27, 3 dc in 6th ch from hook (*first 5 chs count as first dc and ch-2*), *[sk next 2 chs, 3 dc in next ch] twice,

sk next 2 chs, (3 dc, ch 3, 3 dc) in next ch**, [sk next 2 chs, 3 dc in next ch] twice, sk next 2 chs, **dc dec** (*see Stitch Guide*) in next 3 chs, sk next 4 chs, dc dec in next 3 chs, rep from * across, ending last rep at **, [sk next 2 chs, 3 dc in next ch] 3 times, sk next 2 chs, dc in last ch, turn.

Row 2: Ch 1, sk first st, (sc, ch 4, **puff st**—*see Special Stitch*) in first dc in each of next 4 dc groups, *(sc, ch 4, puff st) in next ch-3 sp, (sc, ch 4, puff st) in first dc of each of next 3 dc groups**, sc in each of next 2 dec, (sc, ch 4, puff st) in first dc of each of next 3 dc groups, rep from * across, ending last rep at **, (sc, ch 4, puff st) in first dc of next dc group, sc in last st, turn.

Row 3: Ch 1, sl st in next ch-4 sp, ch 3, *3 dc in each of next 3 ch-4 sps, (3 dc, ch 3, 3 dc) in next ch-4 sp, 3 dc in each of next 2 ch-4 sps**, dc dec in next 2 ch-4 sps, 3 dc in each of next 2 ch-4 sps, rep from * across, ending last rep at **, 3 dc in next ch-4 sp, dc in last ch-4 sp, turn.

Rep rows 2 and 3 alternately for pattern. ∎

Pleasure

PATTERN NOTES
This uses 1 color.

Chain-4 at beginning of row or round counts as first double crochet and chain-1 unless otherwise stated.

Chain-3 at beginning of row or round counts as first double crochet unless otherwise stated.

SPECIAL STITCH
Puff stitch (puff st): [Yo, insert hook as indicated in instructions, yo, pull lp through] 3 times, yo, pull through all lps on hook.

INSTRUCTIONS
Row 1 (RS): Ch a multiple of 39 plus 41, dc in 4th ch from hook (*first 3 chs count as first dc*), dc in next ch, *[ch 1, sk next 2 chs, dc in each of next 2 chs] 3 times, ch 1, sk next 2 chs, (2 dc, ch 3, 2 dc) in next ch, ch 1, sk next 2 chs, dc in next 2 chs, [ch 1, sk next 2 chs, dc in each of next 2 chs] 3 times**, ch 1, sk next 2 chs, **dc dec** (*see Stitch Guide*) in next 2 chs, sk next 2 chs, dc dec in next 2 chs, rep from * across, ending last rep at **, sk next ch, ch 1, sk next 2 chs, dc in each of last 3 chs, turn.

Row 2: Ch 4 (*see Pattern Notes*), *[**puff st** (*see Special Stitch*) in next ch-1 sp, ch 1] 4 times, (puff st, ch 3, puff st) in next ch-3 sp, ch 1, [puff st in next ch-1 sp, ch 1] 4 times**, dc dec in next 2 ch-1 sps, ch 1, rep from * across, ending last rep at **, dc in last st, turn.

Row 3: Ch 3 (*see Pattern Notes*), sk next ch-1 sp, 2 dc in next ch-1 sp, [ch 1, 2 dc in next ch-1 sp] 3 times, *ch 1, (2 dc, ch 3, 2 dc) in next ch-3 sp, [ch 1, 2 dc in next ch-1 sp] 4 times**, ch 1, dc dec in next 2 ch-1 sps, [ch 1, 2 sc in next ch-1 sp] 4 times, rep from * across, ending last rep at **, dc in last st, turn.

Rep rows 2 and 3 alternately for pattern. ∎

Sweet Dreams

PATTERN NOTES
This uses 2 colors.

Join with slip stitch as indicated unless otherwise stated.

Chain-2 at beginning of row or round **does not** count as first stitch unless otherwise stated.

Chain-3 at beginning of row or round counts as first double crochet unless otherwise stated.

INSTRUCTIONS
Row 1 (RS): With first color, ch a multiple of 30 plus 32, dc in 3rd ch from hook (*first 2 chs do not count as first st*), *dc in each of next 13 chs, 3 dc in next ch, dc in each of next 13 chs**, **dc dec** (*see Stitch Guide*) in next 3 chs, rep from * across, ending last rep at **, dc dec in last 2 sts, turn.

Row 2: Ch 1, **sc dec** (*see Stitch Guide*) in first 2 sts, *[tr in next st, sc in next st] 6 times, tr in next st, (sc, tr, sc) in next st, [tr in next st, sc in next st] 6 times, tr in next st**, sc dec in next 3 sts, rep from * across, ending last rep at **, sc dec in last 2 sts, turn.

Row 3: **Ch 2** (*see Pattern Notes*), dc in next st, *dc in each of next 13 sts, 3 dc in next st, dc in each of next 13 sts**, dc dec in next 3 sts, rep from * across, ending last rep at **, dc dec in last 2 sts, turn.

Row 4: Rep row 2.

Row 5: Rep row 3. Fasten off.

Row 6: Join next color with sc in first st, [ch 3, sk next 2 sts, sc in next st] 4 times, *ch 3, sk next 2 sts, ch 3, (sc, ch 3, sc) in next st, [ch 3, sk next 2 sts, sc in next st] 4 times**, ch 2, sk next 2 sts, dc in next st, ch 2, sk next 2 sts, sc in next st, [ch 3, sk next 2 sts, sc in next st] 3 times, rep from * across, ending last rep at **, ch 3, sc in last st, turn.

Row 7: **Ch 3** (*see Pattern Notes*), [sc in next ch-3 sp, ch 3] 5 times, *(sc, ch 3, sc) in next ch-3 sp, [ch 3, sc in next ch-3 sp] 4 times**, ch 3, sc dec in next ch-3 sp, next dc and next ch-3 sp, ch 3, [sc in next ch-3 sp, ch 3] 4 times, rep from * across, ending last rep at **, ch 3, sc in last ch-3 sp, turn.

Row 8: Ch 2, [sc in next ch-3 sp, ch 3] 5 times, *(sc, ch 3, sc) in next ch-3 sp, [ch 3, sc in next ch-3 sp] 4 times**, ch 2, sc dec in next 2 ch-3 sps, ch 2, [sc in next ch-3 sp, ch 3] 4 times, rep from * across, ending last rep at **, ch 1, sl st in 2nd ch of turning ch, turn. Fasten off.

Row 9: **Join** (*see Pattern Notes*) first color in first st, ch 2, 2 dc in next ch-3 sp, *3 dc in each of next 9 ch-3 sps, dc in next ch-3 sp**, dc dec in same ch sp and next ch-3 sp, dc in same ch sp, rep from * across, ending last rep at **, dc dec in same ch sp and last st, turn.

Rep rows 2–9 consecutively for pattern, ending with row 8. ■

Captivating

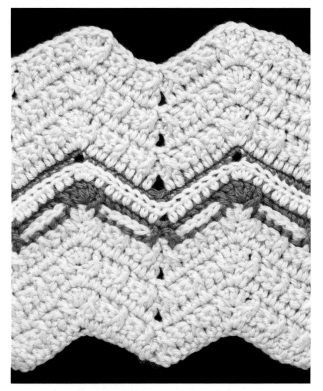

PATTERN NOTES
This uses 3 colors.

Join with slip stitch as indicated unless otherwise stated.

Chain-3 at beginning of row or round counts as first double crochet unless otherwise stated.

Chain-2 at beginning of row or round counts as first half double crochet unless otherwise stated.

INSTRUCTIONS
Row 1 (WS): With first color, ch a multiple of 17 plus 19, dc in 4th ch from hook (*first 3 chs count as first dc*), dc in each of next 6 chs, *3 dc in next ch, dc in each of next 7 chs**, sk next 2 chs, dc in each of next 7 chs, rep from * across, ending last rep at **, dc in last ch, turn.

Row 2 (RS): **Ch 3** (*see Pattern Notes*), sk next st, ***fpdc** (*see Stitch Guide*) around next st, [**bpdc** (*see Stitch Guide*) around each of next 2 sts, fpdc around next st] twice, 3 dc in next dc, fpdc around next dc, [bpdc around each of next 2 dc, fpdc around next st] twice**, sk next 2 sts, rep from * across, ending last rep at **, sk next dc, dc in last st, turn.

Row 3: Ch 3, sk next fpdc, dc in each of next 7 sts, *3 dc in next st, dc in each of next 7 sts**, sk next 2 sts, dc in each of next 7 sts, rep from * across, ending last rep at **, sk next st, dc in last st, turn.

Rows 4–6: [Rep rows 2 and 3 alternately] twice, ending last rep with row 2. At end of last row, fasten off.

Row 7: With RS facing, **join** (*see Pattern Notes*) next color in first st, ch 3, sk next st, *fpdc around next st, bpdc around each of next 5 sts, fpdc around next st, 3 dc in next st, fpdc around next st, bpdc around each of next 5 sts, fpdc around next st**, sk next 2 sts, rep from * around, ending last rep at **, sk next st, dc in last st, **do not turn**. Fasten off.

Row 8: With RS facing, join next color in first st, **ch 2** (*see Pattern Notes*), sk next st, hdc in each of next 7 sts, *3 hdc in next st, hdc in each of next 7 sts**, sk next 2 sts, hdc in each of next 7 sts, rep from * across, ending last rep at **, sk next st, hdc in last st, do not turn. Fasten off.

Row 9: With RS facing and working in **back lps** (*see Stitch Guide*), join 2nd color in first st, ch 1, **sc dec** (*see Stitch Guide*) in same st and next st, sc in each of next 7 sts, *3 sc in next st, sc in each of next 7 sts**, sk next 2 sts, sc in each of next 7 sts, rep from * across, ending last rep at **, sc dec in last 2 sts, turn. Fasten off.

Row 10: With WS facing, working in both lps, join first color in first st, ch 3, sk next st, dc in each of next 7 sts, *3 dc in next st, dc in each of next 7 sts**, sk next 2 sts, dc in each of next 7 sts, rep from * across, ending last rep at **, sk next st, dc in last st, turn.

Rep rows 2–10 consecutively for pattern, ending with row 6. ∎

Fanciful

PATTERN NOTES
This uses 2 colors.

Join with slip st as indicated unless otherwise stated.

Chain-3 at beginning of row or round counts as first double crochet unless otherwise stated.

SPECIAL STITCH
Puff stitch (puff st): [Yo, insert hook as indicated in instructions, yo, pull lp through] 3 times, yo, pull through all lps on hook.

INSTRUCTIONS
Row 1 (WS): With first color, ch a multiple of 12 plus 14, sc in 2nd ch from hook and in each of next 3 chs, *sk next 2 chs, 6 dc in next ch, sk next 2 chs**, sc in each of next 7 chs, rep from * across, ending last rep at **, sc in each of last 4 chs, turn.

Row 2: Ch 1, sc in first st, *sk next 3 sts, **puff st** (see Special Stitch) in next dc, [ch 2, puff st in next dc] 5 times, sk next 3 sc**, sc in next sc, rep from * across, ending last rep at **, sc in last sc, turn. Fasten off.

Row 3: Join (see Pattern Notes) next color in first st, **ch 3** (see Pattern Notes), 2 dc in same st, *sc in next ch-2 sp, [ch 3, sk next ch-2 sp, sc in next ch-2 sp] twice, sk next puff st**, 6 dc in next st, rep from * across, ending last rep at **, 3 dc in last st, turn.

Row 4: Ch 3, dc in same st, [ch 2, puff st in next dc] twice, ch 1, *sk next ch-3 sp, sc in next sc, ch 1, sk next ch-3 sp, ch 1, puff st in next dc**, [ch 2, puff st in next dc] 5 times, ch 1, rep from * across, ending last rep at **, ch 2, puff st in next dc, ch 2, 2 dc in last st, turn. Fasten off.

Row 5: Join first color in first st, ch 3, sk next ch-2 sp, sc in next ch-2 sp, *sk next puff st, 6 dc in next sc, sc in next ch-2 sp**, [ch 3, sk next ch-2 sp, sc in next ch-2 sp] twice, rep from * across, ending last rep at **, ch 3, sk next ch sp, sc in last st, turn.

Row 6: Ch 1, sc in first st, *sk next ch-3 sp and next sc, puff st in next dc, [ch 2, puff st in next dc] 5 times, sk next ch-3 sp**, sc in next sc, rep from * across, ending last rep at **, sc in last st, turn.

Rep rows 3–6 consecutively for pattern. ∎

Sweetheart

PATTERN NOTES
This uses 3 colors.

Join with slip stitch as indicated unless otherwise stated.

Chain-4 at beginning of row or round counts as first double crochet and chain-1 unless otherwise stated.

SPECIAL STITCH
Heart: Sl st around post of next dc, (sc, hdc, tr, hdc, sc, sl st) around same post, ch 3, turn, (sc, hdc, tr, dc, sl st) around post of previously made dc.

INSTRUCTIONS
Row 1 (RS): With first color, ch a multiple of 20 plus 24, 2 dc in 5th ch from hook, *[ch 1, sk next ch, dc in next ch] 3 times, sk next 2 chs, dc in each of next 2 chs, sk next 2 chs, [dc in next ch, ch 1, sk next ch] 3 times**, 2 dc in next ch, ch 2, 2 dc in next ch, rep from * across, ending last rep at **, (2 dc, ch 1, dc) in last ch, turn.

Row 2: Ch 4 (see Pattern Notes), 2 dc in next ch-1 sp, *sk next dc, [ch 1, dc in next ch-1 sp] 3 times, sk next dc, dc in each of next 2 dc, sk next dc, [ch 1, dc in next ch-1 sp] 3 times**, (2 dc, ch 2, 2 dc) in next ch-2 sp, rep from * across, ending last rep at **, (2 dc, ch 1, dc) in last ch-1 sp, turn. Fasten off.

Row 3: Join (see Pattern Notes) next color in first st, ch 4, 2 dc in next ch-1 sp, *[ch 1, dc in next ch-1 sp] 3 times, dc in next dc, heart (see Special Stitch), dc in next dc on this row, [ch 1, dc in next ch-1 sp] 3 times**, (2 dc, ch 2, 2 dc) in next ch-2 sp, rep from * across, ending last rep at **, (2 dc, ch 1, dc) in last ch-1 sp, turn.

Row 4: Ch 4, 2 dc in next ch-1 sp, *[ch 1, dc in next ch-1 sp] 3 times, sk next dc, dc in each of next 2 dc, sk next dc, [ch 1, dc in next ch-1 sp] 3 times**, (2 dc, ch 2, 2 dc) in next ch-2 sp, rep from * across, ending last rep at **, (2 dc, ch 1, dc) in last ch-1 sp, turn. Fasten off.

Row 5: Join next color in first st, ch 4, 2 dc in next ch-1 sp, *sk next dc, [ch 1, dc in next ch-1 sp] 3 times, sk next dc, dc in each of next 2 dc, sk next dc, [ch 1, dc in next ch-1 sp] 3 times**, (2 dc, ch 2, 2 dc) in next ch-2 sp, rep from * across, ending last rep at **, (2 dc, ch 1, dc) in last ch-1 sp, turn.

Row 6: Rep row 2.

Rep rows 3–6 consecutively for pattern, working 2 rows of each color. ■

Wrap It Up

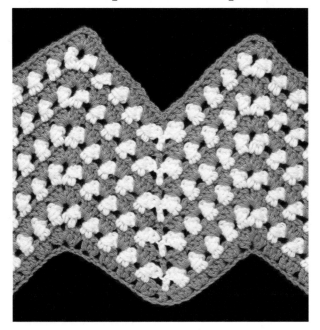

PATTERN NOTES
This uses 2 colors.

Join with slip stitch as indicated unless otherwise stated.

Chain-3 at beginning of row or round counts as first double crochet unless otherwise stated.

SPECIAL STITCH
Wrap: 2 dc as indicated in instructions, dc around post of both sts.

INSTRUCTIONS
Row 1 (RS): With first color, ch a multiple of 30 plus 32, 3 dc in 5th ch from hook, *[sk next 2 chs, 3 dc in next ch] 3 times, sk next 2 chs, (3 dc, ch 2, 3 dc) in next ch, [sk next 2 chs, 3 dc in next ch] 4 times**, sk next 2 chs, dc in next ch, sk next 2 chs, 3 dc in next ch, rep from * across, ending last rep at **, sk next 2 chs, dc in last ch, turn. Fasten off.

Row 2: **Join** *(see Pattern Notes)* next color in first st, **ch 3** *(see Pattern Notes)*, *[sk next st, **wrap**— *see Special Stitch* in next 2 sts, ch 1] 4 times, sk next 2 sts, wrap in next st and ch-3 sp, ch 3, wrap in same ch-3 sp and next st, ch 1, sk next 2 sts, wrap in next 2 sts, [ch 1, sk next st, wrap in next 2 sts] 3 times, sk next st**, dc in next single dc, sk next st, rep from * across, ending last rep at **, dc in last st, turn. Fasten off.

Row 3: Join first color in first st, ch 3, *[sk next wrap, 3 dc in sp between sk wrap and next wrap] 4 times, (3 dc, ch 3, 3 dc) in next ch-3 sp, [sk next wrap, 3 dc in sp between sk wrap and next wrap] 4 times**, dc in next single dc, rep from * across, ending last rep at **, dc in last st, turn.

Rep rows 2 and 3 alternately for pattern. ∎

Daisy Wheels

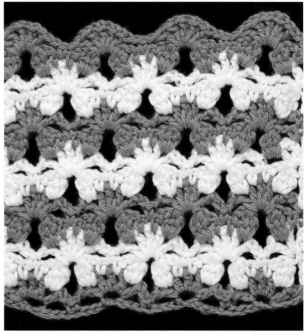

PATTERN NOTES
This uses 2 colors.

Join with slip stitch as indicated unless otherwise stated.

Chain-3 at beginning of row or round counts as first double crochet unless otherwise stated.

Chain-4 at beginning of row or round counts as first double crochet and chain-1 unless otherwise stated.

SPECIAL STITCH
Cluster (cl): Holding back last lp of each st on hook, 3 dc as indicated in instructions, yo, pull through all lps on hook.

INSTRUCTIONS
Row 1 (RS): With first color, ch a multiple of 8 plus 11, sc in 2nd ch from hook, ch 1, *sc in next ch, ch 1, sk next 3 chs, (dc, {ch 1, dc} 4 times) in next ch, ch 1, sk next 3 chs, rep from * across, ending with sc in last st. Fasten off.

Row 2: Join (see Pattern Notes) next color in first st, **ch 3** (see Pattern Notes), *cl (see Special Stitch) in next ch-1 sp, ch 1, [sc in next ch-1 sp, ch 1] twice, cl in next ch-1 sp**, ch 3, sk next ch-1 sp, next sc, and next ch-1 sp, rep from * across, ending last rep at **, dc in last st, turn.

Row 3: Ch 4 (see Pattern Notes), (dc, ch 1, dc) in same st, ch 1, sc in next ch-1 sp between sc, ch 1, *(dc, {ch 1, dc} 4 times) in next ch-3 sp between cls, ch 1, sc in next ch-1 sp between sc, rep from * across, ending with (dc, {ch 1, dc} twice) in last st, turn. Fasten off.

Row 4: Join first color with sc in first st, sc in next ch-1 sp, ch 1, cl in next ch-1 sp, *ch 3, sk next ch-1 sp, next sc and next ch-1 sp, cl in next ch-1 sp, ch 1, [sc in next ch-1 sp, ch 1] twice, cl in next ch-1 sp, rep from * across, ending with ch 3, sk next ch-1 sp, next sc, and next ch-1 sp, cl in next ch-1 sp, ch 1, sc in last ch-1 sp, sc in last st, turn.

Row 5: Ch 1, sc in first st, *ch 1, (dc, {ch 1, dc} 4 times) in next ch-3 sp between next 2 cls, ch 1**, sc in next ch-1 sp between next 2 sc, rep from * across, ending last rep at **, sc in last st, turn. Fasten off.

Rep rows 2–5 consecutively for pattern. ∎

Highs & Lows

PATTERN NOTES
This uses 3 colors.

Join with slip stitch as indicated unless otherwise stated.

Chain-3 at beginning of row or round counts as first double crochet unless otherwise stated.

INSTRUCTIONS
Row 1 (RS): With first color, ch a multiple of 19 plus 22, 2 dc in 4th ch from hook, 3 dc in next ch, *sk next ch, [dc in next ch, sk next ch] 7 times**, 3 dc in each of next 4 chs, rep from * across, ending last rep at **, 3 dc in each of last 2 chs, turn. Fasten off.

Row 2 (WS): Join (see Pattern Notes) next color in first st, **ch 3** (see Pattern Notes), 2 dc in same st, 3 dc in next st, *sk next st, [dc in next st, sk next st] 7 times**, 3 dc in each of next 4 sts, rep from * across, ending last rep at **, 3 dc in each of last 2 sts, turn. Fasten off.

Next rows: Rep row 2 in color sequence of 1 row of each color, beg with 3rd color. ∎

Puff Peaks

PATTERN NOTES
This uses 1 color.

Chain-2 at beginning of row or round **does not** count as first stitch unless otherwise stated.

SPECIAL STITCHES
Puff stitch (puff st): [Yo, insert hook as indicated in instructions, yo, pull lp through] 4 times, yo, pull through all lps on hook.

Decrease (dec): Holding back last lp of each st on hook, dc in next ch or st, sk next 3 chs or as indicated in instructions, dc in next ch or st, yo, pull through all lps on hook.

INSTRUCTIONS
Row 1 (RS): Ch a multiple of 23 plus 24, dc in 3rd ch from hook (*first 2 chs count as first dc*), *[ch 1, sk next ch, dc in next ch] 4 times, ch 1, sk next ch, (dc, ch 1, **puff st**—*see Special Stitches*, ch 2, puff st, ch 1, dc) in next ch,

[ch 1, sk next ch, dc in next ch] 4 times**, ch 1, **dec** (*see Special Stitches*), rep from * across, ending last rep at **, ch 1, sk next ch, **dc dec** (*see Stitch Guide*) in last 2 chs, turn.

Row 2: Ch 2 (*see Pattern Notes*), dc in next dc, *[ch 1, dc in next dc] 4 times, ch 1, (dc, ch 1, puff st, ch 2, puff st, ch 1, dc) in next ch-2 sp, [ch 1, dc in next dc] 4 times**, ch 1, dec, sk dec, rep from * across, ending last rep at **, ch 1, dc dec in last 2 dc, turn.

Rep row 2 for pattern. ■

Here & There

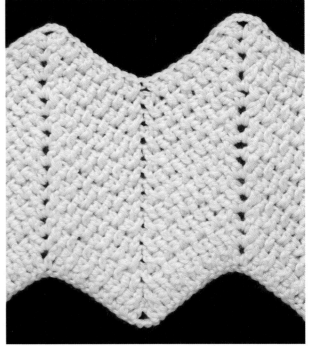

PATTERN NOTES
This uses 1 color.

Chain-3 at beginning of row or round counts as first double crochet unless otherwise stated.

SPECIAL STITCH

Post decrease (post dec): Hold back last lp of each st on hook, dc around st as indicated in instructions, sk next 2 sts or dec, dc around st as indicated in instructions, yo, pull through all lps on hook.

INSTRUCTIONS

Row 1 (RS): Ch a multiple of 26 plus 27, dc in 4th ch from hook, dc in each of next 10 chs, *(dc, ch 3, dc) in next ch, dc in each of next 11 chs**, sk next 3 chs, dc in each of next 11 chs, rep from * across, ending last rep at **, dc in last ch, turn.

Row 2 (WS): **Ch 3** *(see Pattern Notes)*, sk next st, **fpdc** *(see Stitch Guide)* around next st, *[**bpdc** *(see Stitch Guide)* around next st, fpdc around next st] 5 times, (dc, ch 3, dc) in next ch sp, fpdc around next st, [bpdc around next st, fpdc around next st] 4 times, bpdc around next st**, **post dec** *(see Special Stitch)* working fpdc, rep from * across, ending last rep at **, fpdc around next st, sk next st, dc in last st, turn.

Row 3: Ch 2, sk next st, bpdc around next st *(ch-2 and bpdc count as first dec)*, *[fpdc around next st, bpdc around next st] 5 times, (dc, ch 3, dc) in next ch sp, bpdc around next st, [fpdc around next st, bpdc around next st] 4 times, fpdc around next st**, post dec working bpdc, rep from * across, ending last rep at **, bpdc around next st, sk next st, dc in last st, turn.

Next rows: Rep rows 2 and 3 alternately for pattern. ■

Embossed Cheverons

PATTERN NOTES
This uses 1 color.

Chain-3 at beginning of row or round counts as first double crochet unless otherwise stated.

Skip next stitch on this row behind all front post double crochet worked below.

INSTRUCTIONS

Row 1 (RS): Ch a multiple of 10 plus 4, sc in 2nd ch from hook and in each ch across, turn.

Row 2: **Ch 3** *(see Pattern Notes)*, dc in each st across, turn.

Row 3: Ch 1, sc in first st, **fpdc** *(see Stitch Guide)* around next st, [sc in each of next 9 sts, fpdc around next st] across, ending with sc in last st, turn.

Row 4: Rep row 2.

Row 5: Ch 1, sc in first st, fpdc around fpdc below, **sk next st on this row behind fpdc just worked** (*see Pattern Notes*), fpdc around next st on this row, *sc in each of next 7 sts, fpdc around next dc, fpdc around next fpdc below**, fpdc around next dc on this row, rep from * across, ending last rep at **, sc in last st on this row, turn.

Row 6: Rep row 2.

Row 7: Ch 1, sc in first st, fpdc around each of next 2 fpdc below, fpdc around next dc on this row, *sc in each of next 5 sts, fpdc around next dc**, fpdc around each of next 3 fpdc below, fpdc around next dc, rep from * across, ending last rep at **, fpdc around each of next 2 fpdc below, sc in last st, turn.

Row 8: Rep row 2.

Row 9: Ch 1, sc in each of first 2 sts, fpdc around each of next 2 fpdc below, fpdc around next dc, *sc in each of next 3 sts, fpdc around next dc, fpdc around each of next 2 fpdc below**, sc in next st, fpdc around each of next 2 fpdc, fpdc around next dc, rep from * across, ending last rep at **, sc in each of last 2 sts, turn.

Row 10: Rep row 2.

Row 11: Ch 1, sc in each of first 3 sts, *fpdc around each of next 2 fpdc below, fpdc around next dc, sc in next st, fpdc around next dc, fpdc around each of next 2 fpdc below**, sc in each of next 3 sts, rep from * around, ending last rep at **, sc in each of last 3 sts, turn.

Row 12: Rep row 2.

Row 13: Ch 1, sc in each of first 4 sts, *fpdc around each of next 2 fpdc below, fpdc around next dc, fpdc around each of next 2 fpdc below**, sc in each of next 5 sts, rep from * across, ending last rep at **, sc in each of last 4 sts, turn.

Row 14: Rep row 2.

Row 15: Ch 1, sc in first st, *fpdc around next dc, sc in each of next 3 sts, fpdc around each of next 3 fpdc below, sc in each of next 3 sts, rep from * across, ending with fpdc around next dc, sc in last st, turn.

Row 16: Rep row 2.

Row 17: Ch 1, sc in first st, fpdc around next fpdc below, *fpdc around next dc, sc in each of next 3 sts, fpdc around next fpdc below, sc in each of next 3 sts**, fpdc around next dc, fpdc around next fpdc below, rep from * across, ending last rep at **, fpdc around next dc, fpdc around next fpdc, sc in last st, turn.

Row 18: Rep row 2.

Row 19: Rep row 7.

Row 20: Rep row 2.

Row 21: Rep row 9.

Row 22: Rep row 2.

Row 23: Rep row 11.

Row 24: Rep row 2.

Row 25: Rep row 13.

Row 26: Rep row 2.

Next rows: Rep rows 15–26 for pattern. Work the following rows to complete.

LAST ROWS

Row 1: Ch 1, sc in each of first 5 sts, fpdc around each of next 3 fpdc below, [sc in each of next 7 sts, fpdc around each of next 3 fpdc below] across, ending with sc in each of last 5 sts, turn.

Row 2: Rep row 2.

Row 3: Ch 1, sc in first st, fpdc around next dc, [sc in each of next 4 sts, fpdc around next fpdc below] across, ending with sc in last st, turn.

Row 4: Rep row 2.

Row 5: Ch 1, sc in each st across, turn. Fasten off. ■

Cozy Clusters

PATTERN NOTES
This uses 3 colors.

Join with slip stitch as indicated unless otherwise stated.

Chain-3 at beginning of row or round counts as first double crochet unless otherwise stated.

SPECIAL STITCH
Cluster (cl): Holding back last lp of each st on hook, 3 dc as indicated in instructions, yo, pull through all lps on hook.

INSTRUCTIONS
Row 1 (RS): With first color, ch a multiple of 20 plus 22, **cl** (see Special Stitch) in 5th ch from hook, [ch 1, sk next ch, cl in next ch] 3 times, ch 1, sk next ch, *(cl, ch 3, cl) in next ch, [ch 1, sk next ch, cl in next ch] 4 times**, ch 1, sk next 3 chs, [cl in next ch, ch 1, sk next ch] 4 times, rep from * across, ending last rep at **, dc in last st, turn.

Row 2: Ch 3 (see Pattern Notes), sk next cl, *[cl in next ch-1 sp, ch 1] 4 times, (cl, ch 3, cl) in next ch-3 sp, ch 1, [cl in next ch-1 sp, ch 1] 4 times**, sk next 2 cls, rep from * across, ending last rep at **, dc in last st, turn.

Rep row 2 for pattern, working in following color sequence from beg:

Rows 1–5 with first color.

Rows 6 and 7 with 2nd color.

Row 8 with 3rd color.

Rows 9 and 10 with 2nd color. ■

Fringed Fling

PATTERN NOTES
This uses 2 colors.

Join with slip stitch as indicated unless otherwise stated.

Chain-3 at beginning of row or round counts as first double crochet unless otherwise stated.

SPECIAL STITCH
Loop stitch (lp st): Holding 1 x 4-inch piece of craft foam in back, wrap around foam, sc in next st.

INSTRUCTIONS
Row 1 (RS): With first color, ch a multiple of 24 plus 14, 2 dc in 4th ch from hook (*first 3 chs count as first dc*), dc in each of next 9 chs, [**dc dec** (*see Stitch Guide*) in next 5 chs, dc in each of next 9 chs, 5 dc in next ch, dc in each of next 9 chs] across, ending with 3 dc in last st, turn.

Rows 2–4: Ch 3 (*see Pattern Notes*), 2 dc in same st, dc in each of next 9 sts, [dc dec in next 5 sts, dc in each of next 9 sts, 5 dc in next st, dc in each of next 9 sts] across, ending with 3 dc in last st, turn. At end of last row, fasten off.

Row 5: Join next color with sc in first st, sc in each st across, turn.

Row 6: Ch 1, **lp st** (*see Special Stitch*) across, turn. Fasten off.

Row 7: **Join** (*see Pattern Notes*) first color in first st, ch 3, 2 dc in same st, dc in each of next 9 sts, [dc dec in next 5 sts, dc in each of next 9 sts, 5 dc in next st, dc in each of next 9 sts] across, ending with 3 dc in last st, turn.

Rep rows 2–7 consecutively for pattern, ending with row 4. ■

Checkmate

PATTERN NOTES
This uses 3 colors.

Join with slip stitch as indicated unless otherwise stated.

Chain-3 at beginning of row or round counts as first double crochet unless otherwise stated.

Chain-2 at beginning of row or round **does not** count as first stitch unless otherwise stated.

INSTRUCTIONS
Row 1 (RS): With first color, ch a multiple of 32 plus 29, dc in 4th ch from hook (*first 3 chs count as first dc*), dc in next ch, [ch 2, sk next 2 chs, dc in each of next 2 chs] twice, ch 2, sk next 2 chs, (2 dc, ch 3, 2 dc) in next ch, *[ch 2, sk next 2 chs, dc in each of next 2 chs] 3 times**, sk next 2 chs, **dc dec** (*see Stitch Guide*) in next 3 chs, sk next 2 chs, dc in each of next 2 chs, [ch 2, sk next 2 chs, dc in next 2 chs] twice, ch 2, sk next 2 chs, (2 dc, ch 3, 2 dc) in next ch, rep from * across, ending last rep at **, dc in last ch, turn. Fasten off.

Row 2: **Join** (*see Pattern Notes*) next color in first st, **ch 3** (*see Pattern Notes*), [working over next ch-2, dc in each of next 2 sk sts below, ch 2] 3 times, *(2 dc, ch 3, 2 dc) in next ch-3 sp, [ch 2, working over next ch-2, dc in each of next 2 sk sts below] 3 times**, ch 2, sk next ch, dc dec in next 2 chs below, sk next ch, rep from * across, ending last rep at **, ch 2, dc in last st, turn. Fasten off.

Row 3: Working over next ch-2 sp, join next color in first sk st 2 rows below, **ch 2** (*see Pattern Notes*), dc in next dc, [ch 2, working over next ch-2, dc in each of next 2 sk sts 2 rows below] 3 times, *ch 2, (2 dc, ch 3, 2 dc) in next ch-3 sp, [ch 2, working over next ch-2, dc in each of next 2 dc 2 rows below] 3 times**, ch 2, sk next dc below, dc dec in next 2 sk dc below, [ch 2, working over next ch-2, dc in each of next 2 sk dc 2 rows below] 3 times, rep from * across, ending last rep at **, ch 2, dc dec in last 2 dc 2 rows below. Fasten off.

Next rows: Rep row 3 for pattern, working in established color sequence, ending with last color.

Last row: Working over next ch-2, join first color in first sk st 2 rows below, ch 2, dc in next st, *[sc in each of next 2 sts, working over next ch-2, dc in each of next 2 sts 2 rows below] 3 times, sc in each of next 2 sts, 3 sc in next ch-3 sp, [sc in each of next 2 dc, working over ch-2, dc in each of next 2 dc 2 rows below] 3 times, sc in each of next 2 dc**, sk next dc, dc dec in next 2 dc, rep from * across, ending last rep at **, dc dec in last 2 sts 2 rows below. Fasten off. ∎

Filigree Lace

PATTERN NOTES
This uses 2 colors.

Join with slip stitch as indicated unless otherwise stated.

Chain-3 at beginning of row or round counts as first double crochet unless otherwise stated.

SPECIAL STITCH
V-stitch (V-st): (Dc, ch 1, dc) as indicated in instructions.

INSTRUCTIONS
Row 1 (RS): With first color, ch a multiple of 32 plus 32, sc in 2nd ch from hook *ch 1, sk next 2 chs, **V-st** (see Special Stitch) in next ch, ch 1, sk next 2 chs, sc in next ch, ch 1, sk next 2 chs, V-st in next ch, ch 1, sk next 2 chs, sc in next ch, ch 1, sk next 2 chs, (V-st, ch 2, V-st) in next ch, [ch 1, sk next 2 chs, sc in next ch, ch 1, sk next 2 chs, V-st in next ch] twice, ch 1, sk next 2 chs**, **sc dec** (see Stitch Guide) in next 3 chs, rep from * across, ending last rep at **, sc in last ch, turn. Fasten off.

Row 2: Join (see Pattern Notes) next color in first st, **ch 3** (see Pattern Notes), dc in ch sp of next V-st, *[ch 1, V-st in next sc, ch 1, sc in ch sp of next V-st] twice, ch 1, (V-st, ch 2, V-st) in next ch-2 sp, [ch 1, sc in ch sp of next V-st, ch 1, V-st in next sc] twice**, ch 1, sc dec in ch sp of next 2 V-sts, rep from * across, ending last rep at **, ch 1, **dc dec** (see Stitch Guide) in ch sp of last V-st and last st, turn. Fasten off.

Rep row 2 for pattern, working 1 row with each color. ■

Sculpture

PATTERN NOTES
This uses 3 colors.

Do not turn rows; fasten off at end of each row.

Join with slip stitch as indicated unless otherwise stated.

Chain-3 at beginning of row or round counts as first double crochet unless otherwise stated.

SPECIAL STITCH
V-stitch (V-st): (Dc, ch 1, dc) as indicated in instructions.

INSTRUCTIONS
Row 1 (RS): With first color, ch a multiple of 27 plus 31, dc in 4th ch from hook, dc in each of next 2 chs, *[ch 1, sk next ch, dc in each of next 3 chs] twice, ch 1, sk next ch, 3 dc in next ch, ch 3, sk next ch, 3 dc in next ch, [ch 1, sk next ch, dc in each of next 3 chs] twice**, ch 1, sk next ch, [**dc dec** (see Stitch Guide) in next 3 chs] twice, rep from * across, ending last rep at **, ch 1, sk next ch, dc in each of last 3 chs, **do not turn** (see Pattern Notes). Fasten off.

Row 2: Join (see Pattern Notes) next color in first st, **ch 3** (see Pattern Notes), [sk next 3 dc, working over first row, **V-st** (see Special Stitch) in next sk ch, ch 1] 3 times, *sk next 3 dc, (V-st, ch 3, V-st) in next sk ch, [ch 1, V-st in next sk ch] twice**, ch 1, V-st in each of next 2 sk chs, [ch 1, V-st in next sk ch] twice, ch 1, rep from * across, ending last rep at **, ch 1, V-st in next sk ch, dc in last st. Fasten off.

Row 3: With RS facing, join first color in first st, ch 3, holding last row in front of work, working in previous row, *[3 dc in center dc of next dc group, ch 1] 3 times, ch 1, (3 dc, ch 3, 3 dc) in next ch-3 sp at point, [ch 1, 3 dc in center dc of next dc group] 3 times**, dc dec in next 2 dc, ch 1, rep from * across, ending last rep at **, sk next dc group, sl st in last st. Fasten off.

Row 4: With RS facing, join last color in ch-1 sp of V-st below and first st **at same time**, ch 3, *[V-st in ch-1 sp of next V-st below, ch 1] 3 times, ch 1, (V-st, ch 3, V-st) in next ch-3 sp, ch 1, [V-st in ch sp of next V-st below, ch 1] 3 times**, ch 1, dc dec in ch sps of next 2 V-sts, ch 1, rep from * across, ending last rep at **, dc in ch-1 sp of last V-st and last st of previous row at same time. Fasten off.

Row 5: With RS facing, join first color in center dc of first dc group of row behind last row, ch 3, *[3 dc in center dc of next dc group, ch 1] 3 times, (3 dc, ch 3, 3 dc) in next ch-3 sp, [ch 1, 3 dc in center dc of next dc group] 3 times**, ch 1, dc dec in center dc of next dc group and first dc of next dc group, ch 1, rep from * across, ending last rep at **, dc in center dc of next dc group. Fasten off.

Row 6: With RS facing, join first color in ch-1 sp of V-st on last row and last st of previous row **at same time**, ch 3, *[working over ch-1 sp of last row, V-st in ch-1 sp of V-st below, ch 1] 3 times, working over ch-3 sp of last row, (V-st, ch 3, V-st) in next ch-3 sp below, ch 1, [working over ch-1 sp of last row, V-st in ch sp of next V-st below, ch 1] 3 times**, working over ch sp of last row, dc dec in ch-1 sp of next 2 V-sts, ch 1, rep from * across, ending last rep at **, dc in ch-1 sp of last V-st below and last st of previous row at same time. Fasten off.

Row 7: With RS facing, join first color in center dc of first dc group of row behind last row, ch 3, *[3 dc in center dc of next dc group, ch 1] 3 times, (3 dc, ch 3, 3 dc) in next ch-3 sp of previous row at point, [ch 1, 3 dc in center dc of next dc group] 3 times**, ch 1, dc dec in center dc of next 2 dc groups, ch 1, rep from * across, ending last rep at **, dc in center dc of last dc group. Fasten off.

Row 8: With first color, rep row 6.

Row 9: With first color, rep row 7.

Row 10: With first color, rep row 6.

Row 11: With first color, rep row 7.

Rep rows 6–11 consecutively for pattern maintaining color sequence of:

next color;

first color;

last color;

first color for 7 rows;

ending with row 6 and last color. ■

Staccato

PATTERN NOTES
This uses 3 colors.

Join with slip stitch as indicated unless otherwise stated.

Chain-2 at beginning of row or round counts as first double crochet unless otherwise stated.

SPECIAL STITCH
V-stitch (V-st): (Dc, ch 1, dc) as indicated in instructions.

INSTRUCTIONS
Row 1 (RS): With first color, ch a multiple of 26 plus 25, **V-st** (*see Special Stitch*) in 5th ch from hook, [sk next 2 chs, V-st in next ch] twice, sk next 2 chs, *(V-st, ch 3, V-st) in next ch, [sk next 2 chs, V-st in next ch] 3 times**, sk next 2 chs, **dc dec** (*see Stitch Guide*) in next 3 chs, [sk next 2 chs, V-st in next ch] 3 times, sk next 2 chs, rep from * across, ending last rep at **, sk next ch, dc in last ch, turn.

Row 2: **Ch 2** (*see Pattern Notes*), dc in ch sp of first V-st, V-st in ch sp in each of next 3 V-sts, *(V-st, ch 3, V-st) in next ch-3 sp, V-st in ch sp of each of next 3 V-sts**, dc dec in ch sp of next V-st, next dc dec and in ch sp of next V-st, V-st in ch sp of each of next 3 V-sts, rep from * across, ending last rep at **, dc dec in ch sp of last V-st and last st, turn. Fasten off.

Row 3: Join next color with sc in sp between last dc dec and next V-st, [ch 3, sc in sp between next 2 V-sts] 3 times, *ch 3, 3 sc in next ch-3 sp, [ch 3, sc in sp between next 2 V-sts] 3 times**, **sc dec** (*see Stitch Guide*) in sp before and in sp after next dc dec, [ch 3, sc in sp between next 2 V-sts] 3 times, rep from * across, ending last rep at **, ch 3, sc in sp between last V-st and last st, turn. Fasten off.

Row 4: **Join** (*see Pattern Notes*) next color in first st, ch 2, working over last row, dc in ch sp of V-st below, *V-st in each ch sp of next 3 V-sts, (V-st , ch 3, V-st) in ch-3 sp below, V-st in each ch sp of next 3 V-sts below**, dc dec in ch sp of next 2 V-sts below, rep from * across, ending last rep at **, dc dec in ch sp of last V-st below and last st, turn. Fasten off.

Row 5: Join first color in first st, ch 2, dc in ch sp of next V-st, *V-st in each ch sp of next 3 V-sts, (V-st, ch 3, V-st) in next ch-3 sp, V-st in each ch sp of next 3 V-sts**, dc dec in ch sp of next V-st, next dc dec and ch sp of next V-st, rep from * across, ending last rep at **, dc dec in ch sp of last V-st and last st, turn.

Rep rows 2–5 consecutively for pattern, ending with row 3. ∎

Eccentric

PATTERN NOTE
This uses 1 color.

SPECIAL STITCH
Decrease (dec): Insert hook in next ch or st, yo, pull lp through, sk next 2 chs or sts, insert hook in next st, yo, pull lp through, yo, pull through all lps on hook.

INSTRUCTIONS
Row 1 (RS): Ch a multiple of 11 plus 10, sc in 2nd ch from hook, *ch 2, sk next ch, sc in next ch, ch 2, sk next ch, (sc, ch 2, sc) in next ch, ch 2, sk next ch, sc in next ch**, ch 2, sk next ch, **dec** (*see Special Stitch*), rep from * across, ending last rep at **, ch 2, sk next ch, sc in last ch, turn.

Row 2: Ch 1, sk first st, sc in first ch-2 sp, *ch 2, sc in next ch-2 sp, ch 2, (sc, ch 2, sc) in next ch-2 sp**, ch 2, sc in next ch-2 sp, **sc dec** (*see Stitch Guide*) in next 2 ch-2 sps, rep from * across, ending last rep at **, ch 2, sc in next ch-2 sp, ch 2, sc dec in last ch-2 sp and last st, turn.

Rep row 2 for pattern. ∎

Surface Chevrons

INSTRUCTIONS

Row 1 (RS): With first color, ch a multiple of 16 plus 8, sc in 2nd ch from hook and in each ch across, turn.

Row 2: Ch 3 *(see Pattern Notes)*, dc in each st across, turn.

Rows 3–5: Ch 1, sc in each st across, turn.

Rep rows 2–5 consecutively for pattern to desired length, ending last rep with row 3.

CHEVRON TRIM

Row 1: Join *(see Pattern Notes)* next color around post of first dc of 2nd dc row from bottom, ch 1, **fpsc** *(see Stitch Guide)* around same st, ch 6, fpsc around 5th dc of previous dc row, [ch 6, sk next 7 sts on same row as first fpsc, fpsc around next dc, ch 6, sk next 7 sts on previous dc row, fpsc around next st] across, ending with ch 6, fpsc around last st. Fasten off.

Row 2: Rep row 1, working around same dc.

Continue to work 2 rows of Chevron Trim across dc rows as established. ∎

PATTERN NOTES

This uses 2 colors.

Join with slip stitch as indicated unless otherwise stated.

Chain-3 at beginning of row or round counts as first double crochet unless otherwise stated.

STITCH GUIDE

STITCH ABBREVIATIONS

beg	begin/begins/beginning
bpdc	back post double crochet
bpsc	back post single crochet
bptr	back post treble crochet
CC	contrasting color
ch(s)	chain(s)
ch-	refers to chain or space previously made (i.e., ch-1 space)
ch sp(s)	chain space(s)
cl(s)	cluster(s)
cm	centimeter(s)
dc	double crochet (singular/plural)
dc dec	double crochet 2 or more stitches together, as indicated
dec	decrease/decreases/decreasing
dtr	double treble crochet
ext	extended
fpdc	front post double crochet
fpsc	front post single crochet
fptr	front post treble crochet
g	gram(s)
hdc	half double crochet
hdc dec	half double crochet 2 or more stitches together, as indicated
inc	increase/increases/increasing
lp(s)	loop(s)
MC	main color
mm	millimeter(s)
oz	ounce(s)
pc	popcorn(s)
rem	remain/remains/remaining
rep(s)	repeat(s)
rnd(s)	round(s)
RS	right side
sc	single crochet (singular/plural)
sc dec	single crochet 2 or more stitches together, as indicated
sk	skip/skipped/skipping
sl st(s)	slip stitch(es)
sp(s)	space(s)/spaced
st(s)	stitch(es)
tog	together
tr	treble crochet
trtr	triple treble
WS	wrong side
yd(s)	yard(s)
yo	yarn over

YARN CONVERSION

OUNCES TO GRAMS		GRAMS TO OUNCES	
1	28.4	25	⅞
2	56.7	40	1⅔
3	85.0	50	1¾
4	113.4	100	3½

UNITED STATES		UNITED KINGDOM
sl st (slip stitch)	=	sc (single crochet)
sc (single crochet)	=	dc (double crochet)
hdc (half double crochet)	=	htr (half treble crochet)
dc (double crochet)	=	tr (treble crochet)
tr (treble crochet)	=	dtr (double treble crochet)
dtr (double treble crochet)	=	ttr (triple treble crochet)
skip	=	miss

Reverse single crochet (reverse sc): Ch 1, sk first st, working from left to right, insert hook in next st from front to back, draw up lp on hook, yo, and draw through both lps on hook.

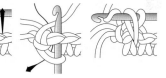

Chain (ch): Yo, pull through lp on hook.

Single crochet (sc): Insert hook in st, yo, pull through st, yo, pull through both lps on hook.

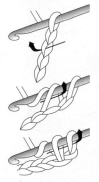

Double crochet (dc): Yo, insert hook in st, yo, pull through st, [yo, pull through 2 lps] twice.

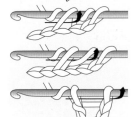

Front loop (front lp) Back loop (back lp)

Front Loop   Back Loop

Front post stitch (fp): Back post stitch (bp): When working post st, insert hook from right to left around post st on previous row.

Back   Front

Post of Stitch

Half double crochet (hdc): Yo, insert hook in st, yo, pull through st, yo, pull through all 3 lps on hook.

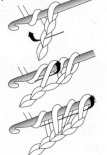

Double treble crochet (dtr): Yo 3 times, insert hook in st, yo, pull through st, [yo, pull through 2 lps] 4 times.

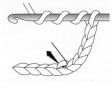

Slip stitch (sl st): Insert hook in st, pull through both lps on hook.

Chain color change (ch color change) Yo with new color, draw through last lp on hook.

Double crochet color change (dc color change) Drop first color, yo with new color, draw through last 2 lps of st.

Treble crochet (tr): Yo twice, insert hook in st, yo, pull through st, [yo, pull through 2 lps] 3 times.

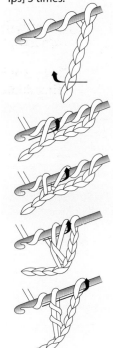

Single crochet decrease (sc dec):
(Insert hook, yo, draw lp through) in each of the sts indicated, yo, draw through all lps on hook.

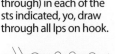
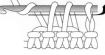

Example of 2-sc dec

Half double crochet decrease (hdc dec):
(Yo, insert hook, yo, draw lp through) in each of the sts indicated, yo, draw through all lps on hook.

Example of 2-hdc dec

Double crochet decrease (dc dec):
(Yo, insert hook, yo, draw lp through, yo, draw through 2 lps on hook) in each of the sts indicated, yo, draw through all lps on hook.

Example of 2-dc dec

Treble crochet decrease (tr dec):
Holding back last lp of each st, tr in each of the sts indicated, yo, pull through all lps on hook.

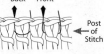

Example of 2-tr dec

Metric Conversion Charts

METRIC CONVERSIONS

yards	x	.9144	=	metres (m)
yards	x	91.44	=	centimetres (cm)
inches	x	2.54	=	centimetres (cm)
inches	x	25.40	=	millimetres (mm)
inches	x	.0254	=	metres (m)

centimetres	x	.3937	=	inches
metres	x	1.0936	=	yards

INCHES INTO MILLIMETRES & CENTIMETRES (Rounded off slightly)

inches	mm	cm	inches	cm	inches	cm	inches	cm
1/8	3	0.3	5	12.5	21	53.5	38	96.5
1/4	6	0.6	5 1/2	14	22	56	39	99
3/8	10	1	6	15	23	58.5	40	101.5
1/2	13	1.3	7	18	24	61	41	104
5/8	15	1.5	8	20.5	25	63.5	42	106.5
3/4	20	2	9	23	26	66	43	109
7/8	22	2.2	10	25.5	27	68.5	44	112
1	25	2.5	11	28	28	71	45	114.5
1 1/4	32	3.2	12	30.5	29	73.5	46	117
1 1/2	38	3.8	13	33	30	76	47	119.5
1 3/4	45	4.5	14	35.5	31	79	48	122
2	50	5	15	38	32	81.5	49	124.5
2 1/2	65	6.5	16	40.5	33	84	50	127
3	75	7.5	17	43	34	86.5		
3 1/2	90	9	18	46	35	89		
4	100	10	19	48.5	36	91.5		
4 1/2	115	11.5	20	51	37	94		

KNITTING NEEDLES CONVERSION CHART

Canada/U.S.	0	1	2	3	4	5	6	7	8	9	10	10½	11	13	15
Metric (mm)	2	2¼	2¾	3¼	3½	3¾	4	4½	5	5½	6	6½	8	9	10

CROCHET HOOKS CONVERSION CHART

Canada/U.S.	1/B	2/C	3/D	4/E	5/F	6/G	8/H	9/I	10/J	10½/K	N
Metric (mm)	2.25	2.75	3.25	3.5	3.75	4.25	5	5.5	6	6.5	9.0

Annie's Attic®

50 Ripple Stitches is published by DRG, 306 East Parr Road, Berne, IN 46711. Printed in USA. Copyright © 2011 DRG.

RETAIL STORES: If you would like to carry this pattern book or any other DRG publications, visit DRGwholesale.com.

Every effort has been made to ensure that the instructions in this publication are complete and accurate.
We cannot, however, take responsibility for human error, typographical mistakes or variations in individual work.
Please visit AnniesCustomerCare.com to check for pattern updates.

ISBN: 978-1-59635-362-6

3 1901 04933 4693

2 3 4 5 6 7 8 9